ELM GREEN PREPARATORY SCHOOL

PRIZE

Awarded to
Frederick Cooper

Maxwell Spence Mathematics Cup and prize for excellent academic achievement

A PASSING ON
OF SHELLS

Poems to share from
Scallywag Press

A PASSING ON OF SHELLS

50 FIFTY-WORD POEMS

BY

SIMON LAMB

ILLUSTRATED BY

CHRIS RIDDELL

Scallywag Press Ltd
LONDON

First published in 2023
by Scallywag Press Ltd
10 Sutherland Row
London, SW1V 4JT

Text © Simon Lamb, 2023
Illustrations © Chris Riddell, 2023

The right of Simon Lamb and Chris Riddell to be identified
as the author and illustrator of this work respectively
has been asserted by them in accordance with Section 77
of the Copyright, Designs and Patents Act, 1988

All rights reserved

Typeset in Charter by the poet

Hand-lettering by the illustrator

Book design and production by Louise Millar

Printed and bound in China on FSC paper
by C&C Offset Printing Co. Ltd

MIX
Paper | Supporting
responsible forestry
FSC® C008047
www.fsc.org

002

British Library Cataloguing in Publication Data available

ISBN 978-1-915252-12-8

Contents

How to Start an Adventure	8
The Scribble	10
Word Count	12
Searching for Ideas	14
Hide and Seek	16
The Basketballer	18
Macaroni Man	20
Which Witch?	22
Hip 'op	24
On the Last Day of Camp	26
Haiku-koo Clock	28
The Bully Henry Greeve	30
Concerning the Very Last Cracker and the Last Slice of Cheese	32
The Satsuma Rumour	34
Fifteen Seconds in the Life of a Goldfish	36
Setting Up a Story	38
Overheard in the Post Office on a Monday Morning	40
The Childhood Thief	42

Wisdom in the Wood	*44*
Pocket Poem	*46*
Medals	*48*
When the Chickens Crossed the Road	*50*
Eulogy for Harry the Hedgehog	*52*
Untitled I: Paint on Canvas	*54*
The Arrogant Letter A	*56*
Garden Phantoms	*58*
Welcome Winter	*60*
The Rainbow in the Cupboard	*62*
On Breakers	*64*
A Line in the Sand	*66*
Happy New Year	*68*
Still Earth	*70*
What We Wear	*72*
The Three-Legged Race	*74*
Golden Retrieval	*76*
Tales from a Garden	*78*
Two Slugs Just Chilling in the Compost Bin	*80*

An Incident in Kingston Hall	82
Murder Mystery	84
You Make Me So ACROSTIC	86
Apocalyptic Scene from an Otherwise Unwritten Story	88
Advice on How to Care for a Fallen Star	90
Return of the Dwellers	92
They Built a Bridge	94
The Sun's Lament	96
Nine Lives of Cat	98
Life on the Rock	100
The Boys at Summer's End	102
What I Know About You	104
Snow Globes	106
Acknowledgements	*108*
About the Poet	*110*
About the Illustrator	*111*
About the Publisher	*112*

How to Start an Adventure

Rise up from the couch.

Go to the living room door.

Open it.

Step into the hallway.

Slip on some sturdy shoes,

    doesn't matter which,

        you choose.

Then go to the front door.

    Open it, too.

Breathe in the view.

Then step outside,

    giving thanks to the sun,

        and run.

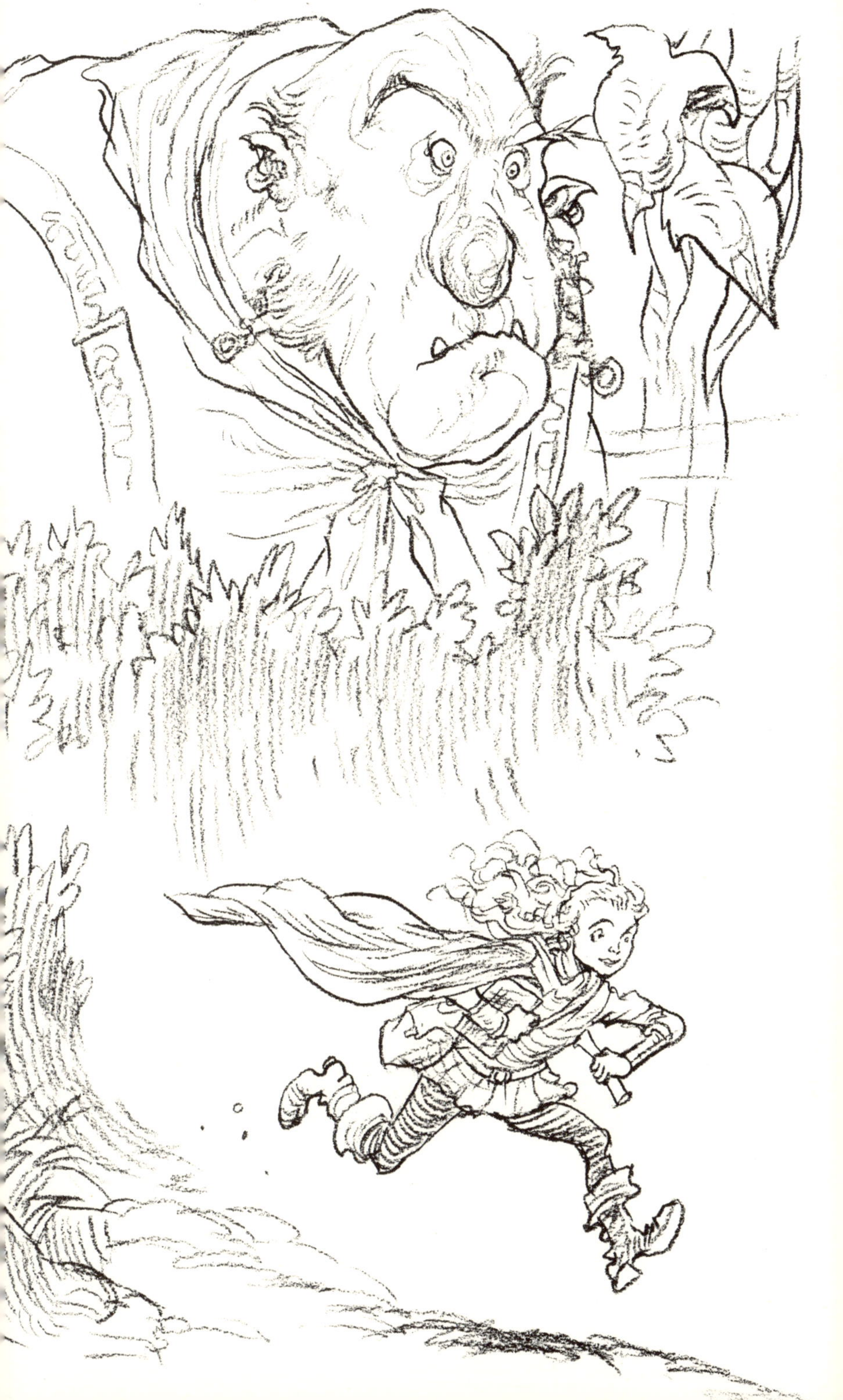

The Scribble

it started as a doodle
a scrawl upon the paper
that looped and curled
and bounced and twirled
and snaked a curvy caper

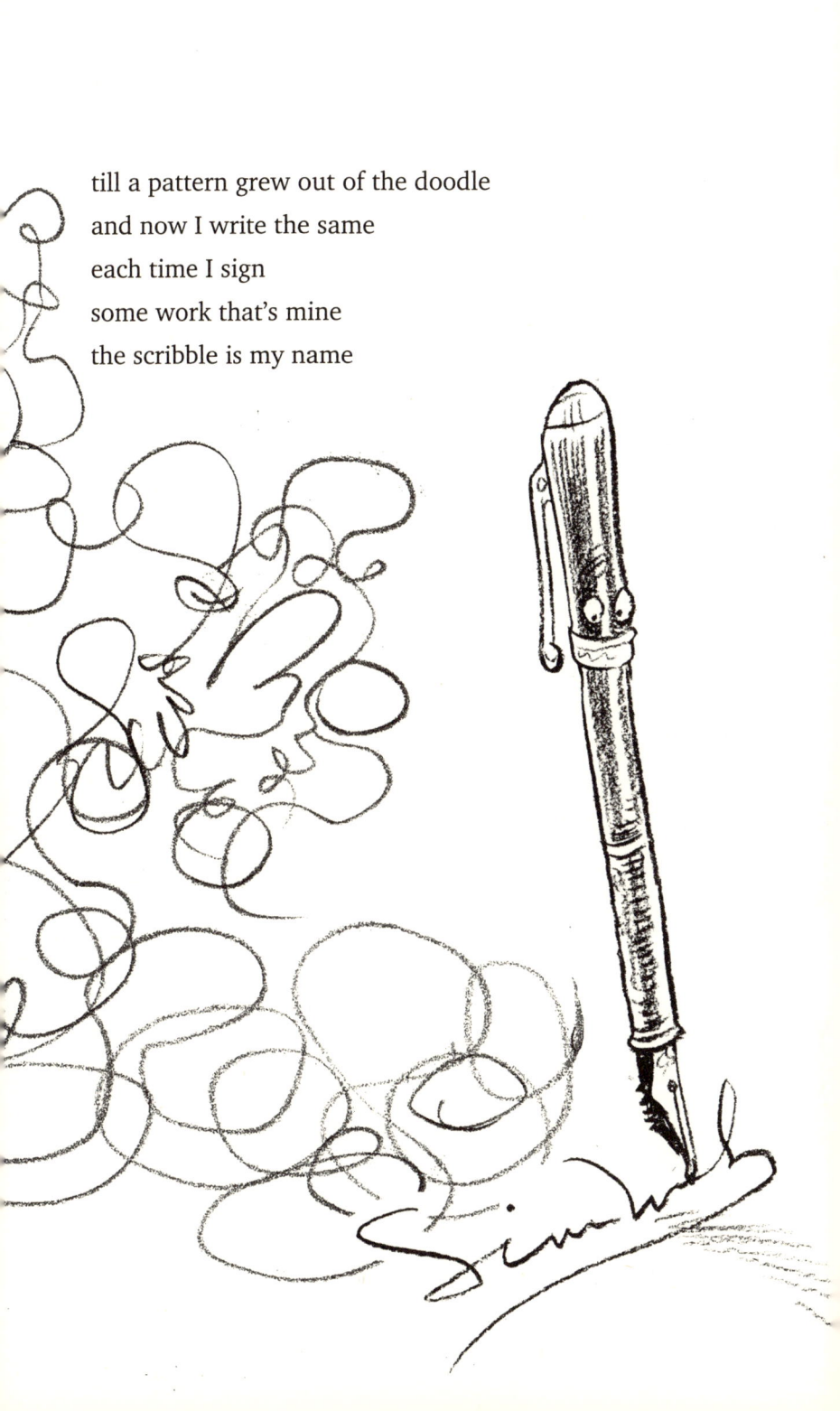

till a pattern grew out of the doodle
and now I write the same
each time I sign
some work that's mine
the scribble is my name

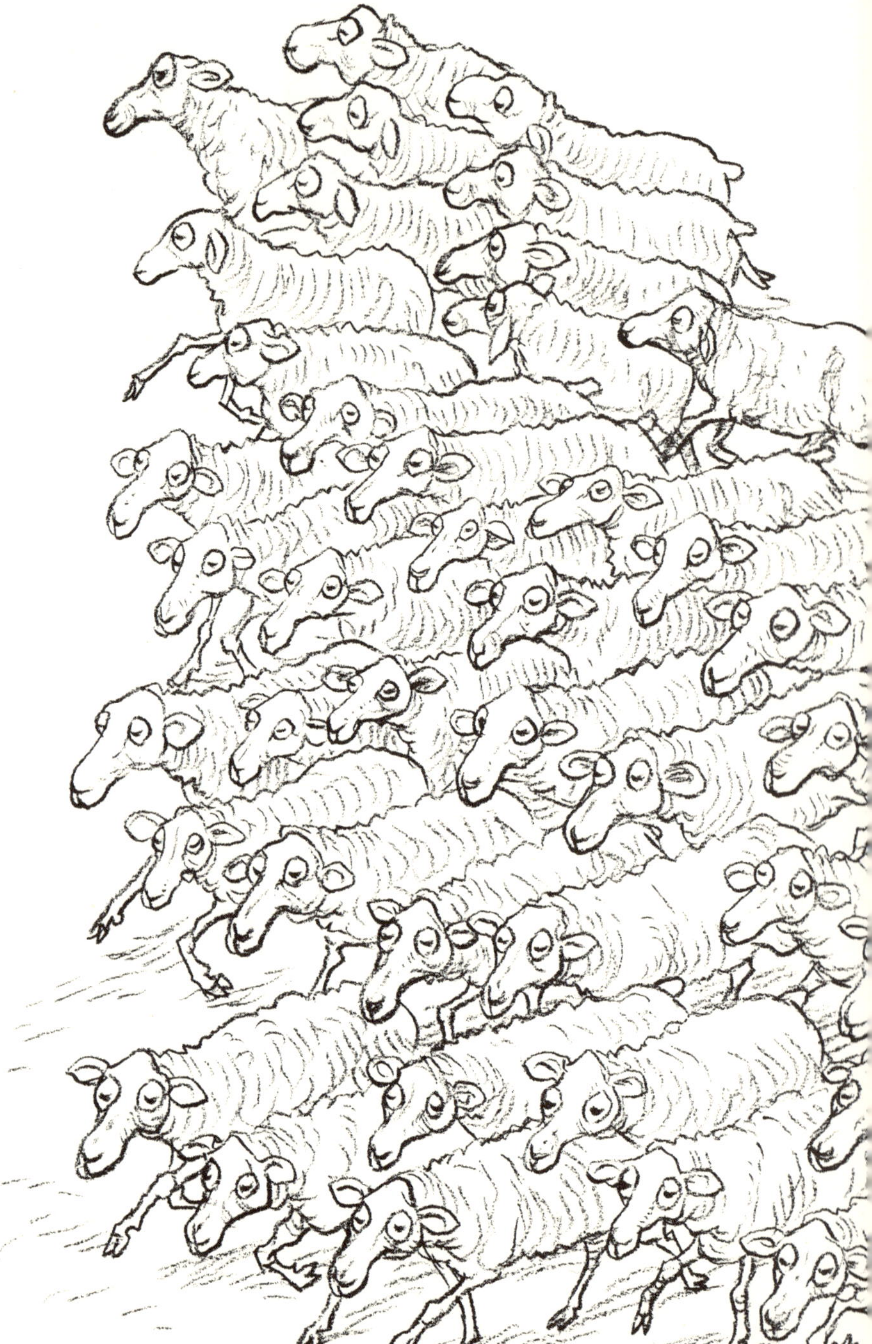

Word Count

My teacher set the word count at exactly fifty words.
The challenge: write a poem. Nothing could be worse!

My rhyming is abysmal
and my metre's sadly dismal

but, my friends, I am a trier so I broke it into thirds
and I wrote this little poem in exactly fifty words.

Searching for Ideas

I glimpsed a glimmer of a great idea
just out of my eye but somewhere near
so I crept over quiet and I didn't dare speak
(having hunted the beast for over a week)
then I readied my pen but alas that was when
the monster took flight once again!

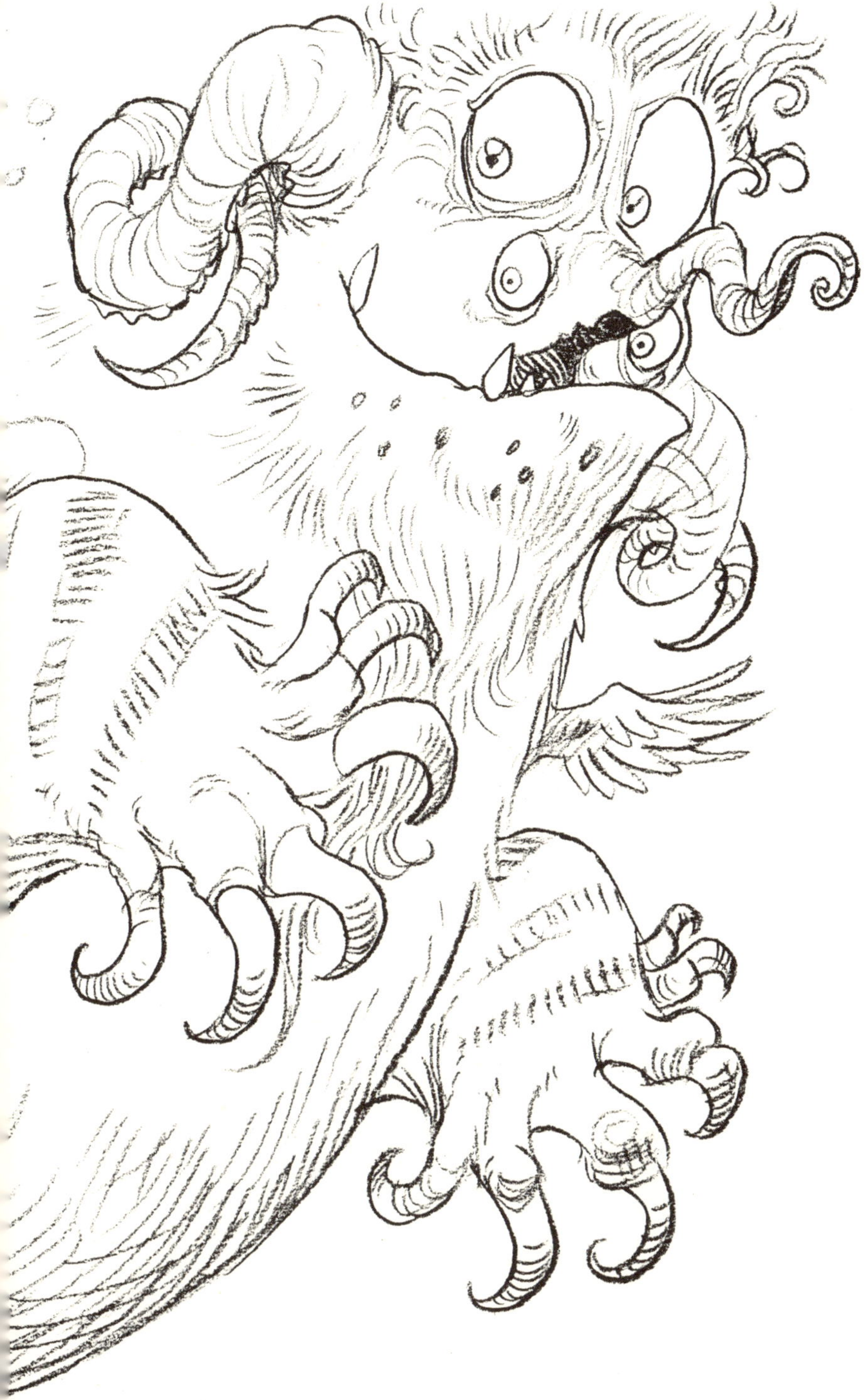

Hide and Seek

Are you in the attic
    where the old toys go?

                              . . . no.

Are you underneath the stairs
    where our watches glow?

                              . . . no.

Are you in the cellar
    hiding down below?

                              . . . no.

Are you in the wardrobe
    behind this pretty lemon dress?

                              . . . no.

Are you in the downstairs loo?

                              BOO!
                          Found you.

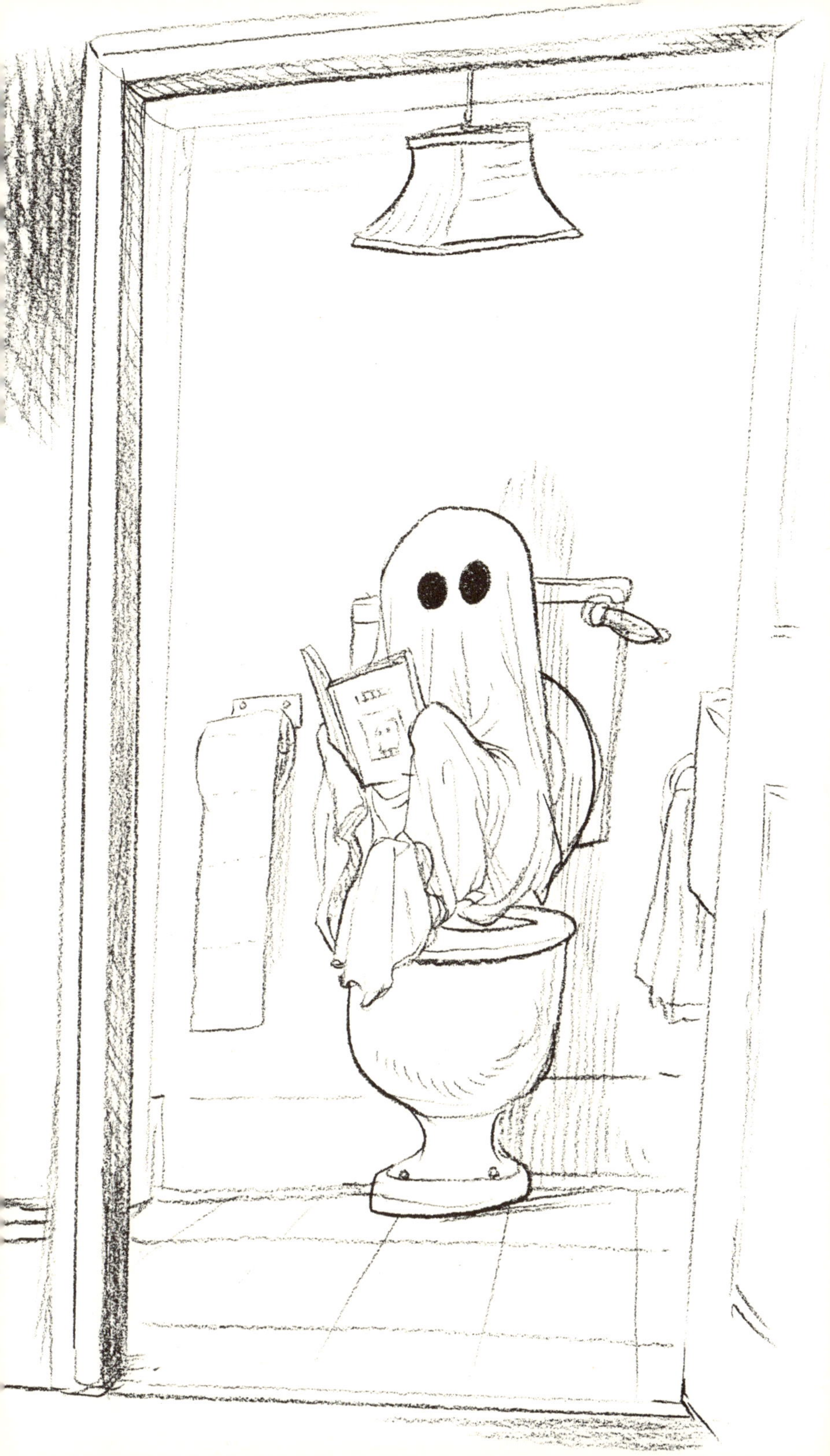

The Basketballer

My little baby brother is a brilliant basketballer
and he's bound to get much better when he's grown a little taller
and although one day he'll shoot the hoop this super pro my sibling
will forget about the days when he was just a baby dribbling

                                                    dribbling

                                                                  dribbling

SLAM DUNK!

Macaroni Man

Let me tell you something . . .

My dad's a pretty brilliant chef,
a knockout kitchen whizz!
Of all the food in all the world,
the best around is his.

I love his macaroni!
Here's the secret of his grub:
he cuts some slits into the lid,
then microwaves the tub!

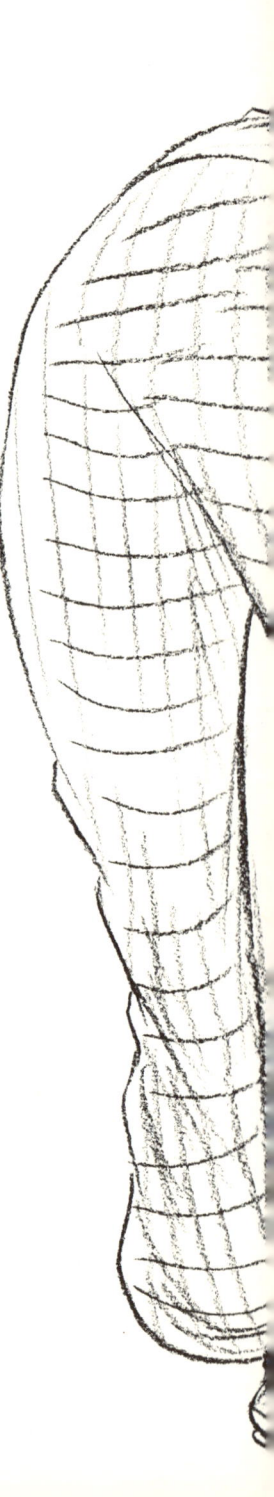

Ping!

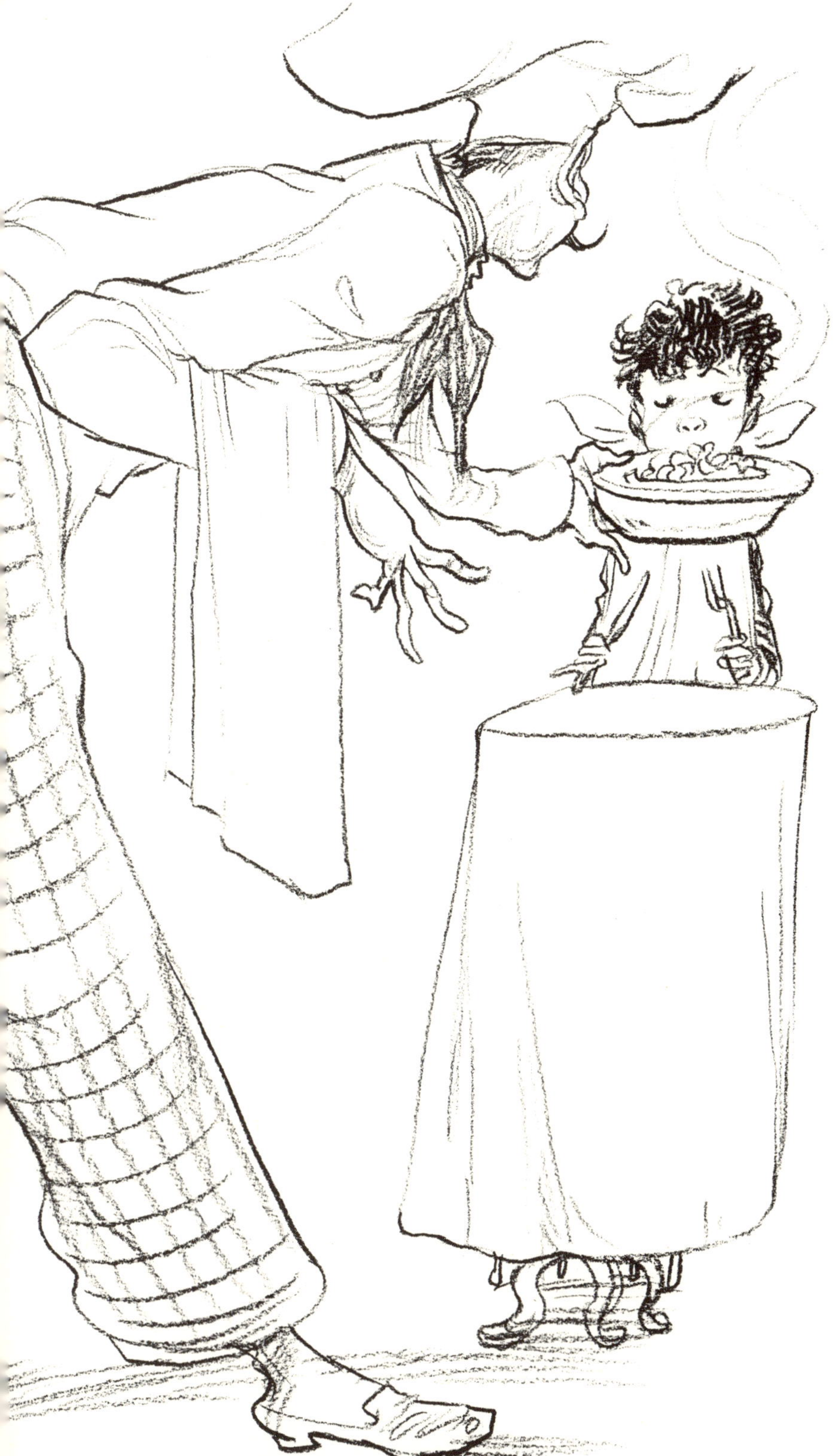

Which Witch?

My daddy is a scaredy cat!
He warns me of the witch:
he says she's got a hairy wart,
a broomstick and a twitch.

He says the very thought of her
leaves him cold and numb.
But at least she's got a friend in me:
I love my mummy's mum!

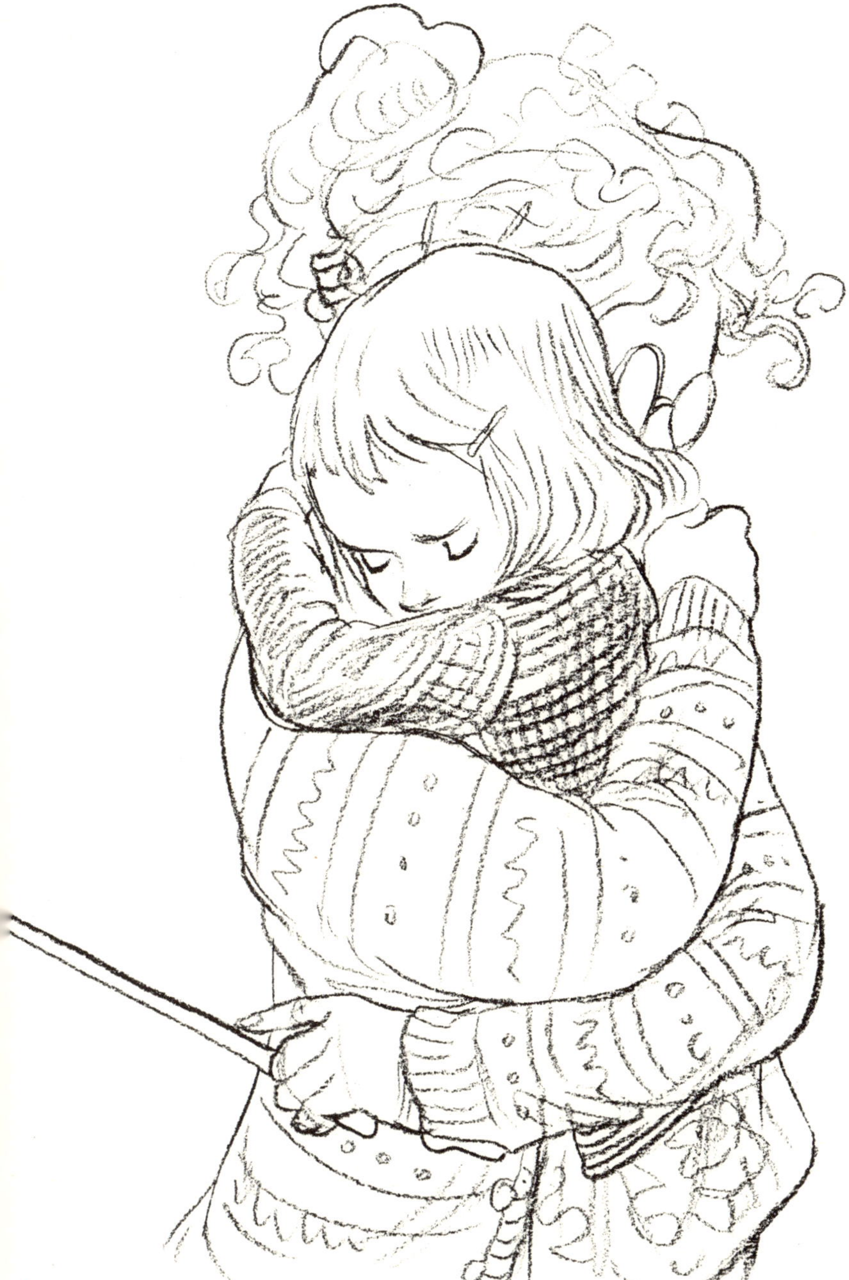

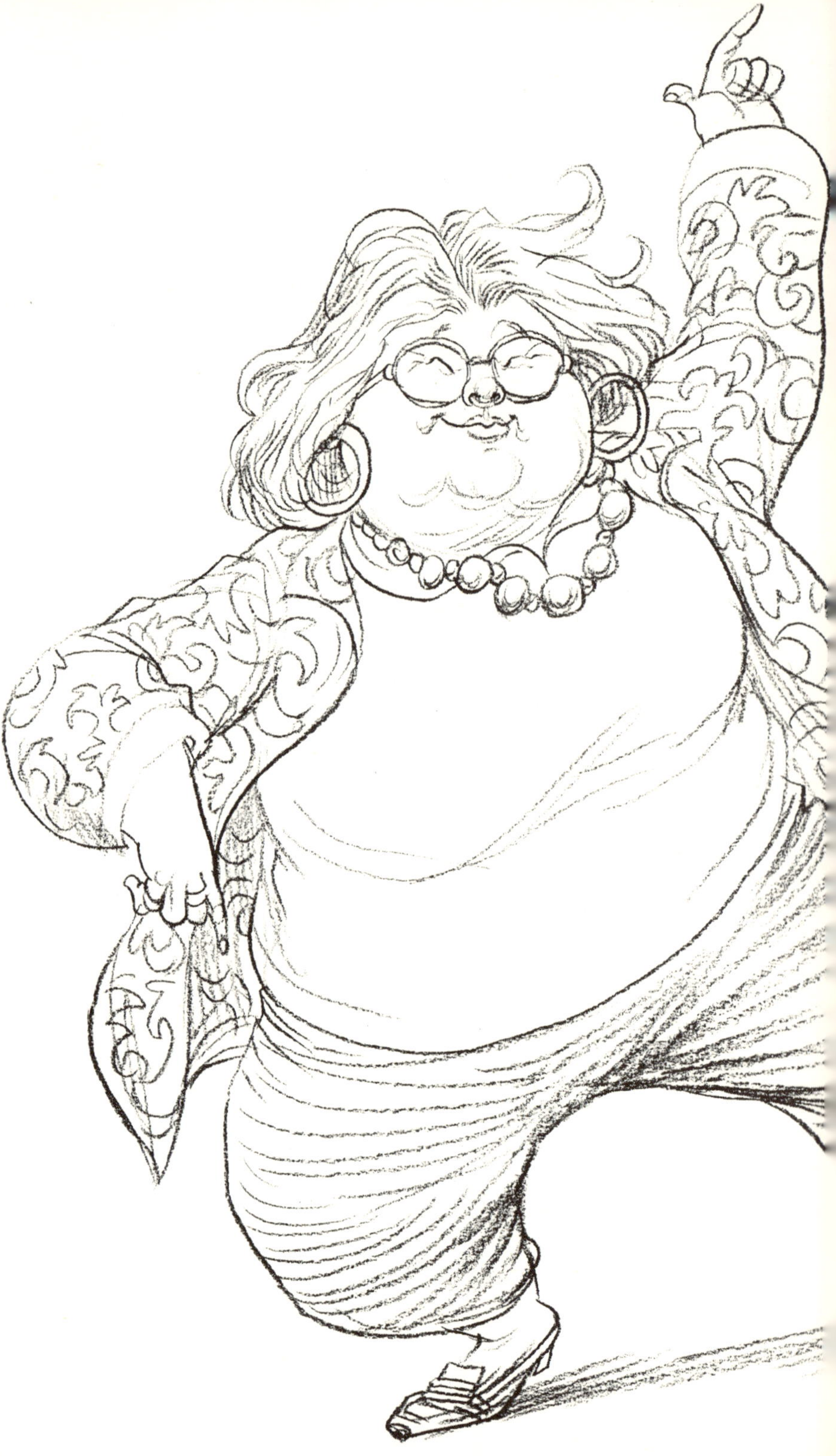

Hip 'op

Granny couldn't dance or bust a move
– she shuffled oh so slow –
until one day she did proclaim,
"These hips have got to go!"

. . . and so . . .

She had some operations
that made her feel nine not ninety-four.
Now just you wait for Friday night:
she'll hip 'op out the door!

On the Last Day of Camp

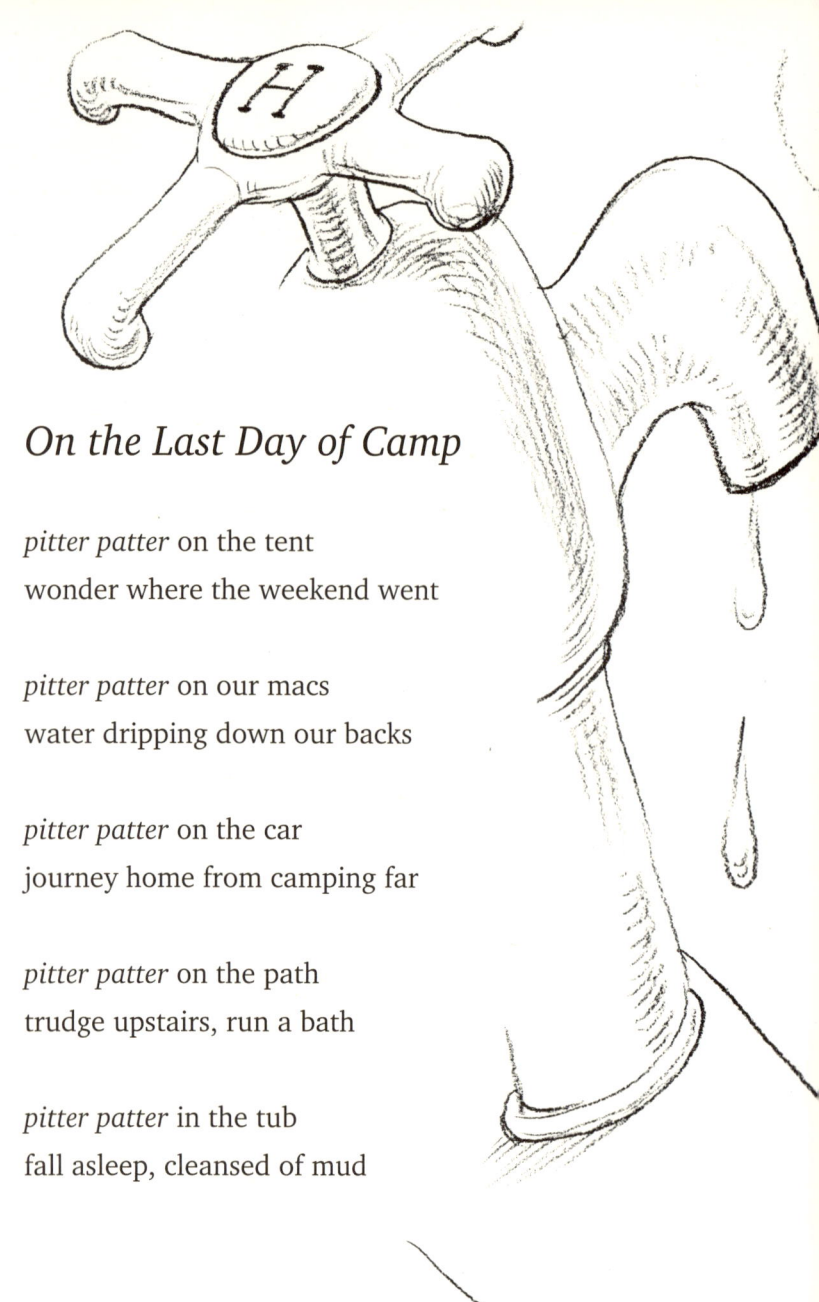

pitter patter on the tent
wonder where the weekend went

pitter patter on our macs
water dripping down our backs

pitter patter on the car
journey home from camping far

pitter patter on the path
trudge upstairs, run a bath

pitter patter in the tub
fall asleep, cleansed of mud

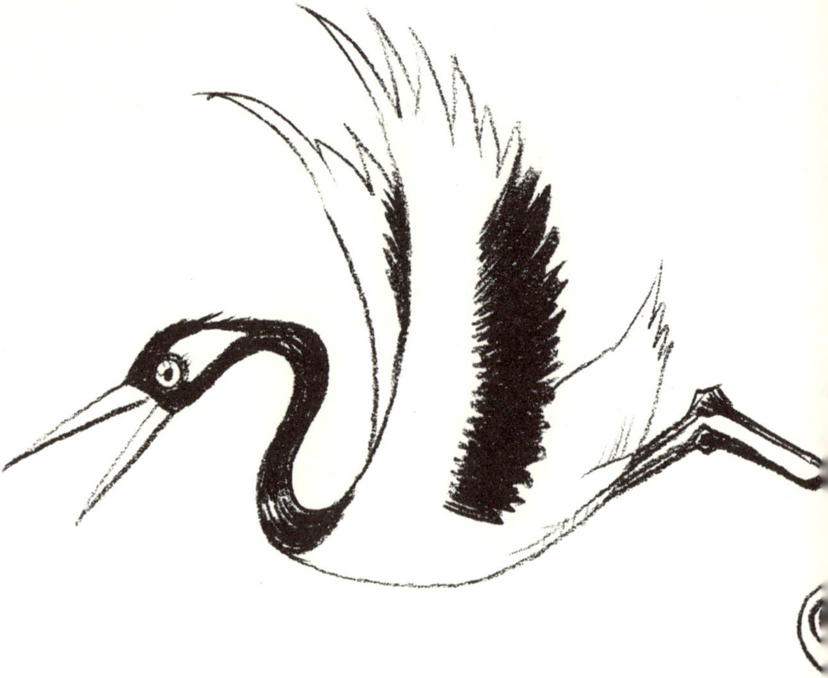

Haiku-koo Clock

one o'clock is here
still the sheep of night do tread
sleep come to my head

two o'clock is here
still I lie awake in bed
read a book instead

three o'clock is here
still the one thing that I dread
the new day dawning

I so hate Monday morning.

The Bully Henry Greeve

Who's the boy who bullies boys?
The bully, Henry Greeve.

Who's the boy who steals their toys?
The bully, Henry Greeve.

Who's the boy destroying joys?
The bully, Henry Greeve.

Who's the boy whose fists enjoy
the bully, Henry Greeve?

He's the boy the boys employ
to bully Henry Greeve.

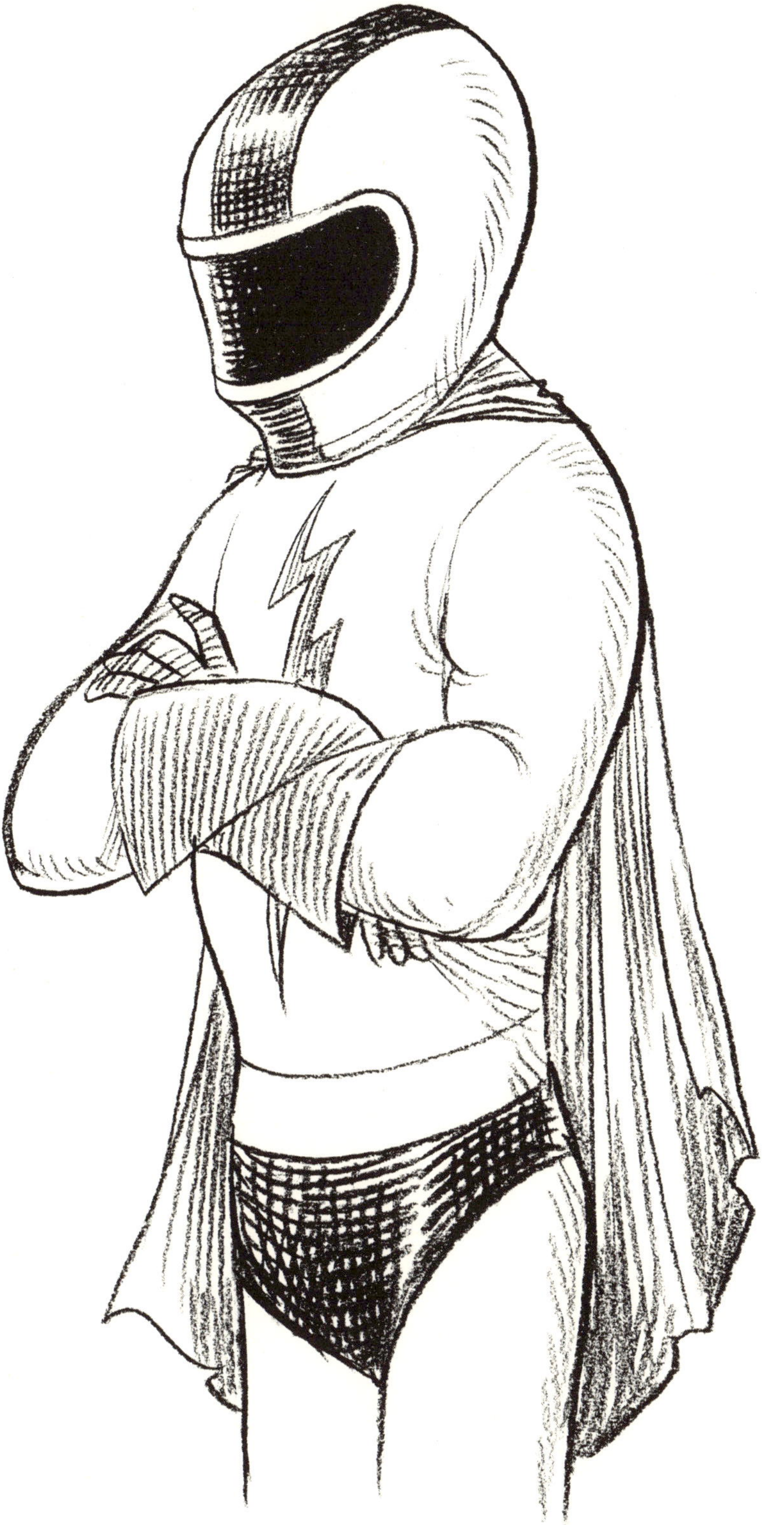

Concerning the Very Last Cracker and the Last Slice of Cheese

The very last cracker sat on the plate.
Mum said to Dad, "Wait.
Perhaps we should break it up into threes
and then do the same with the last slice of cheese?"

Huh!

Thirds in my mouth would be surely a swizz—

—then Steven arrived and shoved them in his!

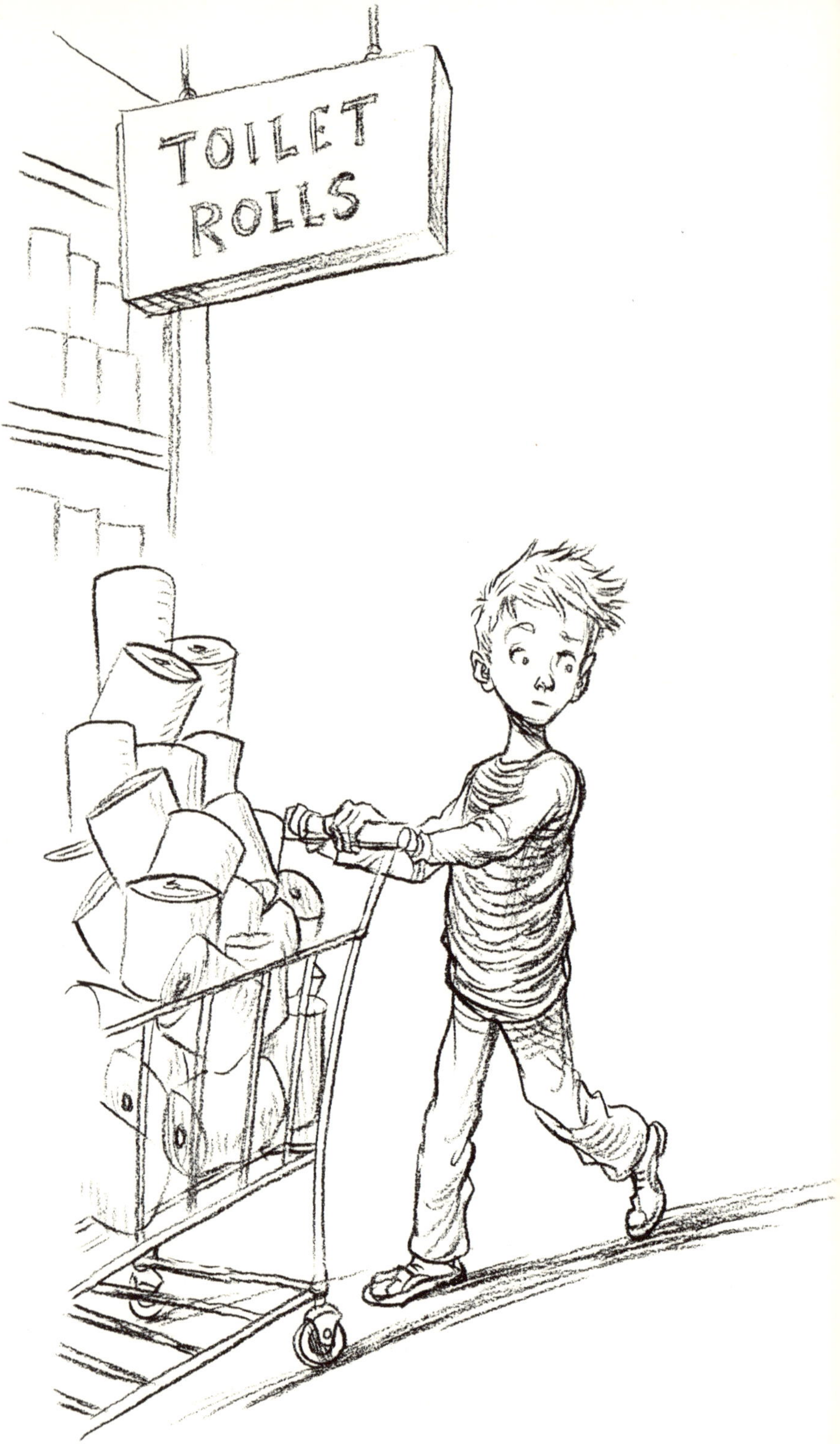
TOILET
ROLLS

The Satsuma Rumour

Have you heard the rumours?
They're rationing satsumas.

>Rationing satsumas?
>I can't believe these rumours.

I've also heard consumers
are fighting for satsumas.

>Fighting for satsumas?!
>Because of silly rumours?

It seems that these consumers
must really love satsumas.

>If they really loved satsumas,
>they'd say bloomers to these rumours!

Fifteen Seconds in the Life of a Goldfish

swim around the goldfish bowl

                      oh look
               a sunken wreck

swim around the goldfish bowl

oh look
a treasure chest

swim around the goldfish bowl

                      oh look
               a sunken wreck

swim around the goldfish bowl

oh look
a treasure chest

swim around the goldfish bowl

            oh look
        a human face

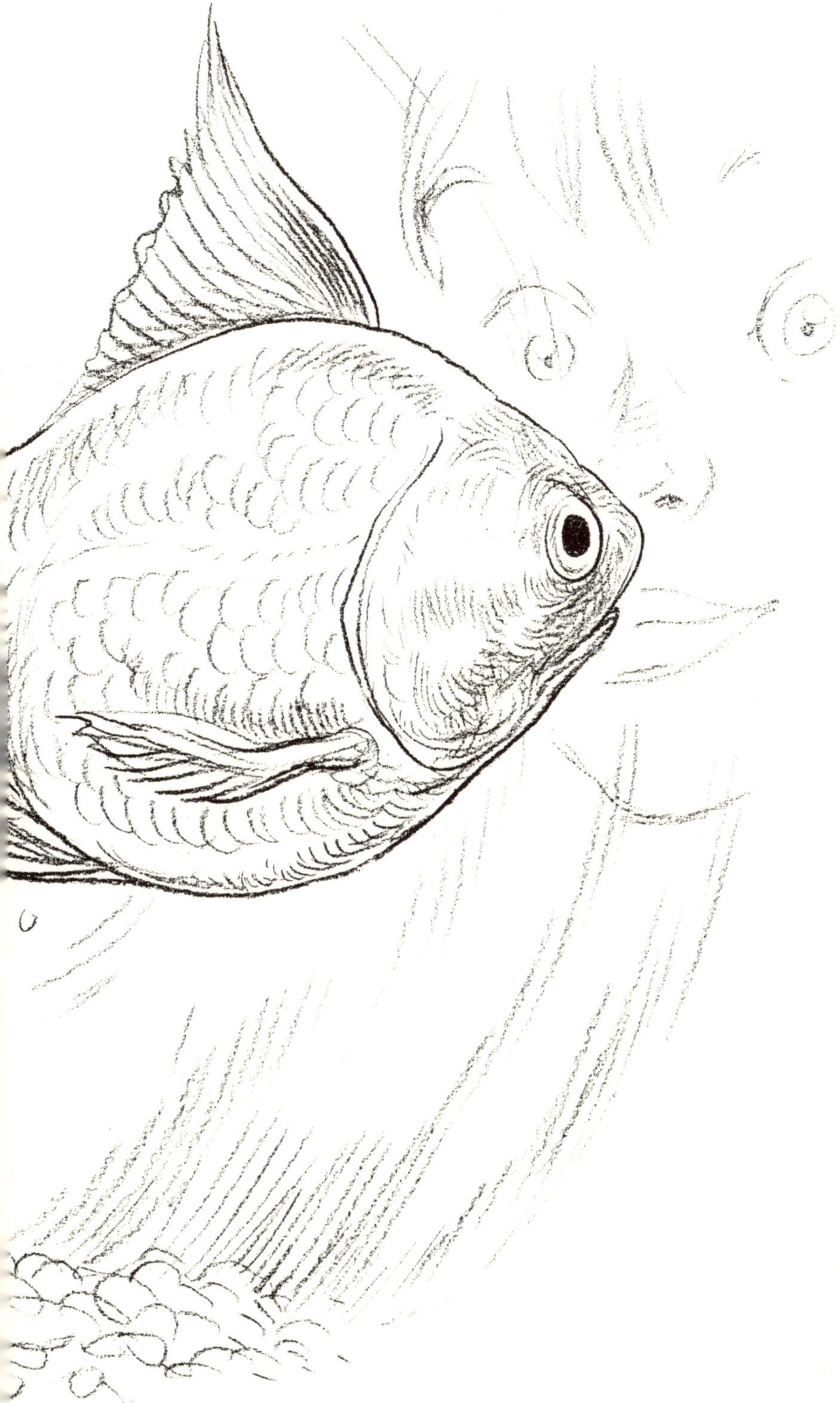

Setting Up a Story

Once upon a time /
right /
there lived these two kids /
curious as mice /
yeah /
and there was this castle /
like, huge /
with these great towers /
and a wooden drawbridge /
and a secret door /
and so much more /
anyway /
these kids lived /
with a wonderful storyteller /
and *Once upon a time* /

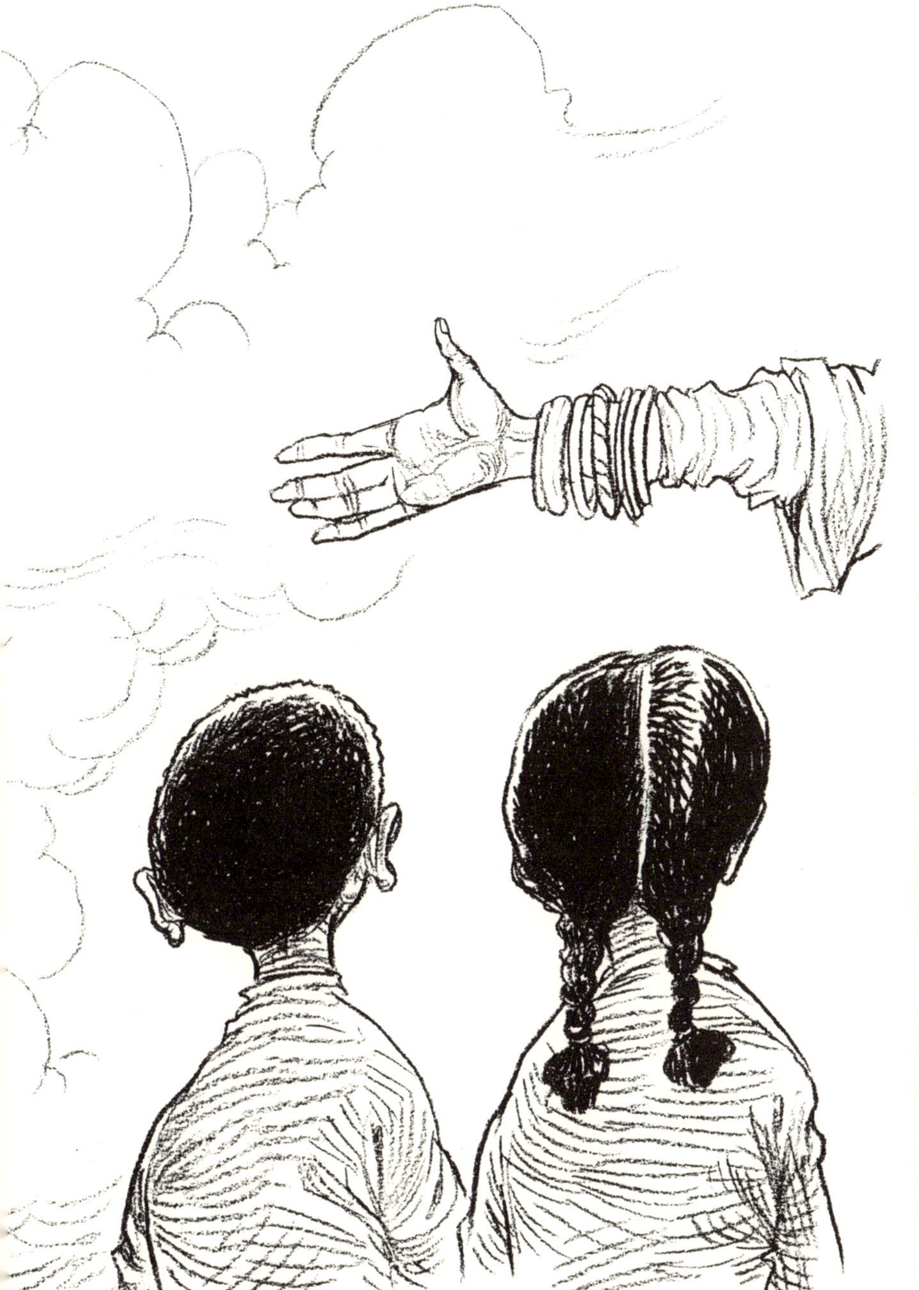

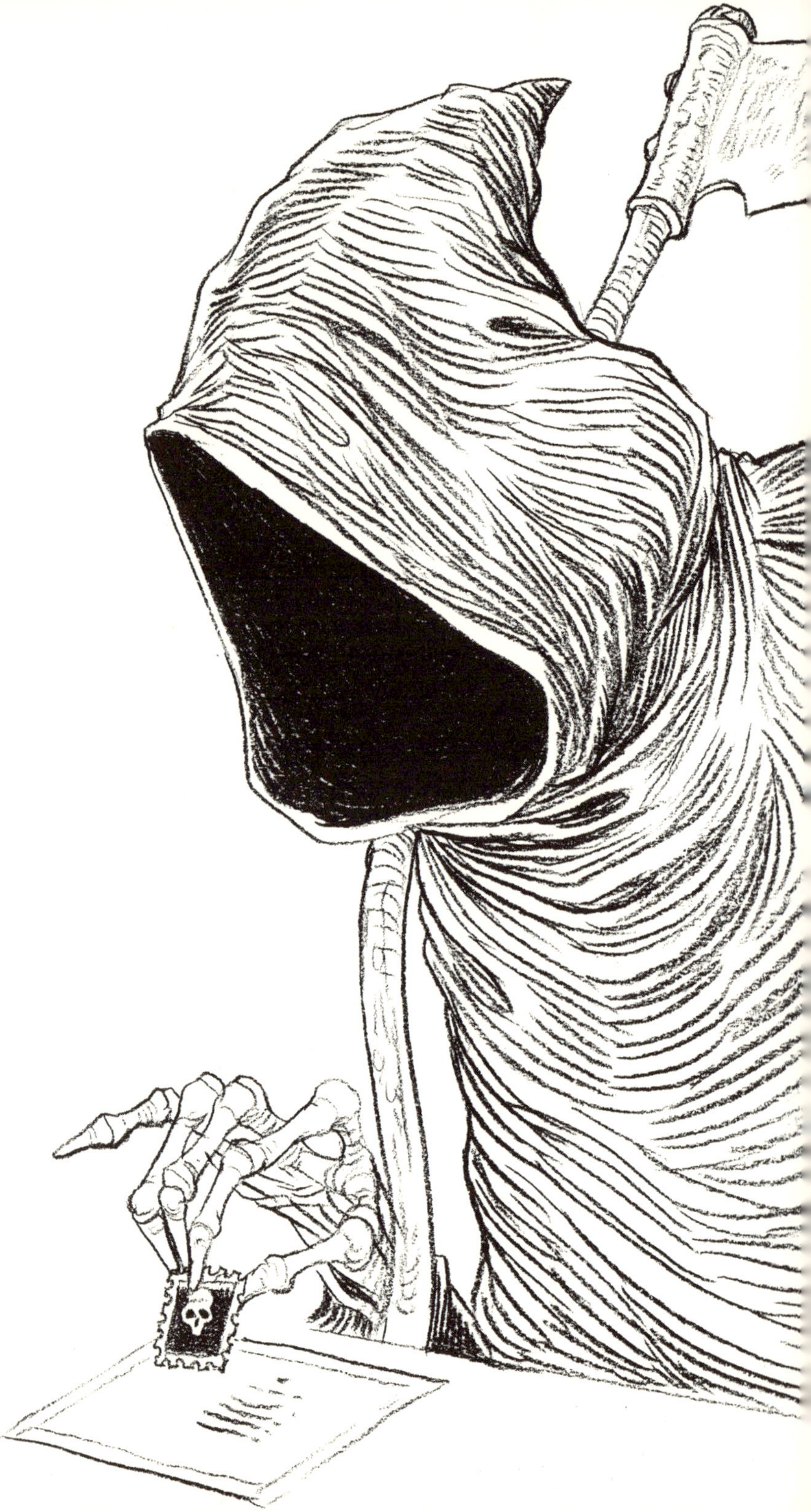

Overheard in the Post Office on a Monday Morning

"Morning, John."

"Morning, Sue."

"I hear that Bernard's got the flu,
Miss Haxby's got a brand new hip,
and Sheena, well, she took a trip.
Robert's ill, and whatshisname
has had to buy a zimmer frame,
and Mr Almond's stuck in bed..."

—then *thump!*

Poor Susan dropped down dead.

"Next!"

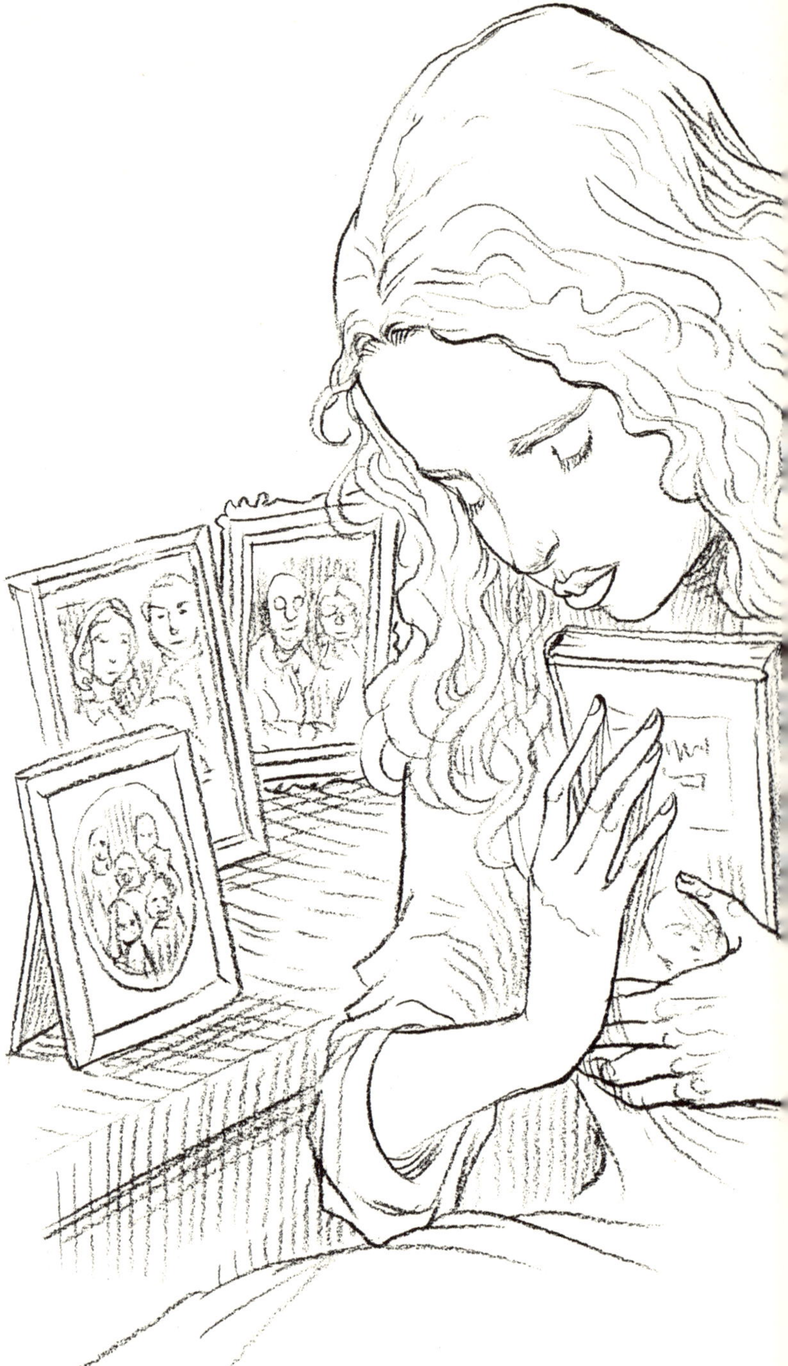

The Childhood Thief

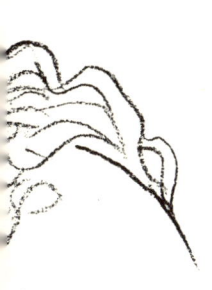

Mummy, look,
> the sky is singing.
>> I need your song.

Daddy, look,
> the clouds are crying.
>> I need your tears.

Granny, look,
> the light is fading.
>> I need your smile.

Grandpa, look,
> the stars are silent.
>> I need your peace.

Poet, look,
> the poem is ending.
>> I need your words.

Wisdom in the Wood

    Obligingly I could
hack through the darking wood
and clear a path for you
to step unhindered through,
to save you from the thorn
and scratches that I've worn.

But, knowing what I know,
instead, I'll let you go,
alone, to forge your track.
    I'll teach you how to hack.

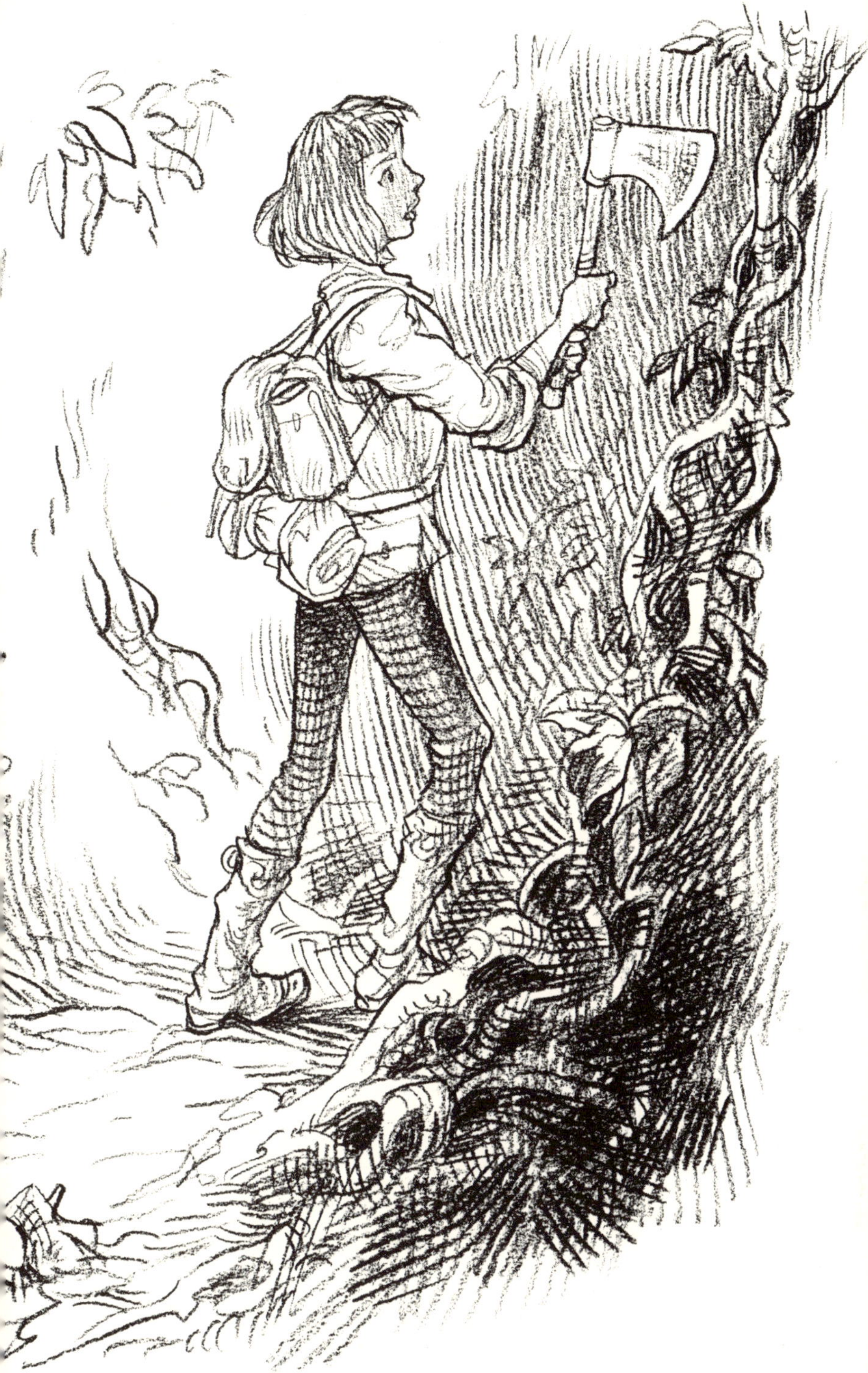

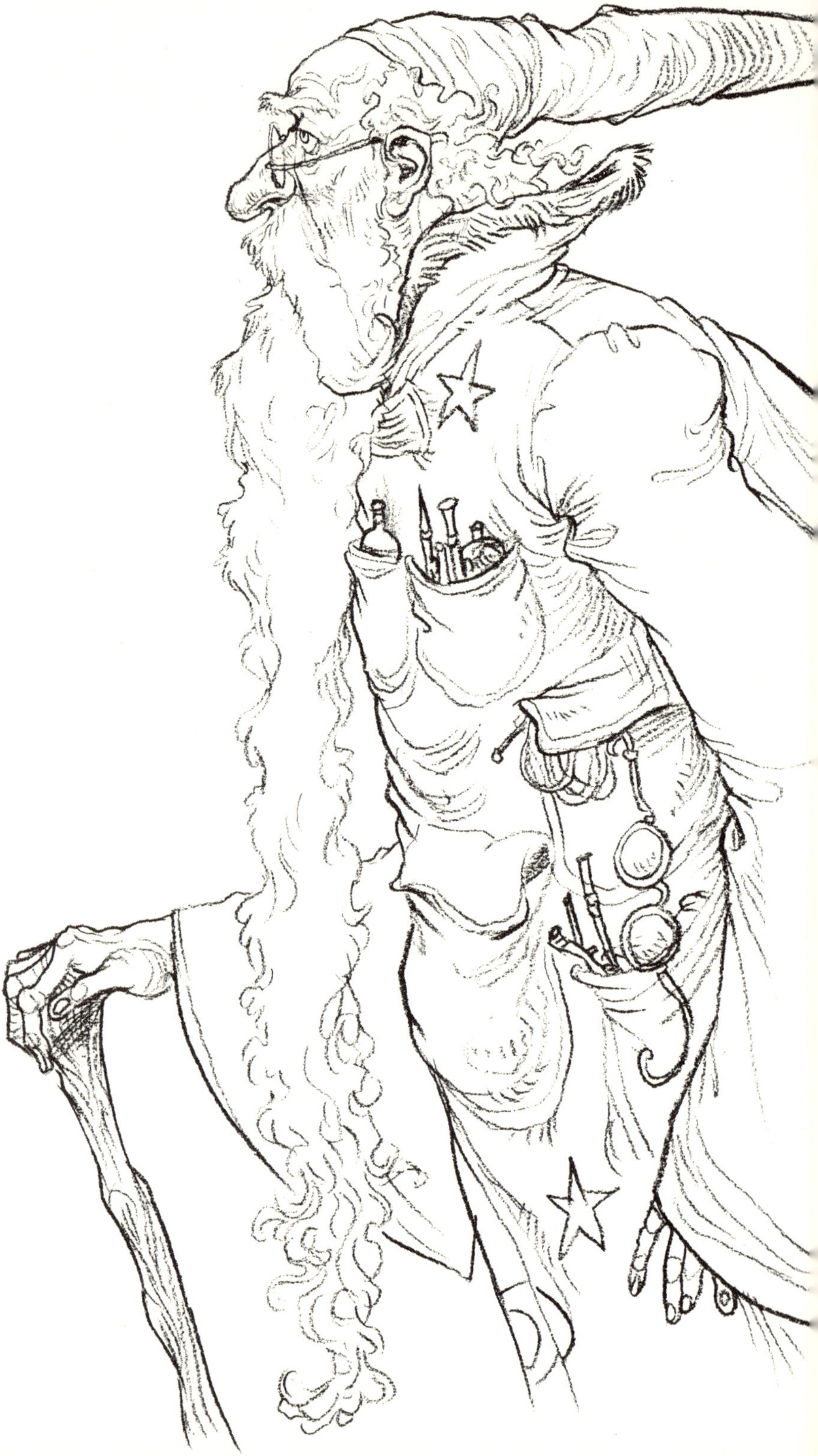

Pocket Poem

I wear a coat with multiple pockets:

> in this one,
> a promise;
>
> in this,
> a curl of sky;
>
> in that one,
> marshmallows for toasting;
>
> here,
> perfect pen, midnight blue.

I'll always wear this coat.
I'll never ever bin it.
Because, you see,
I'm always *me*
whenever I am in it.

Medals

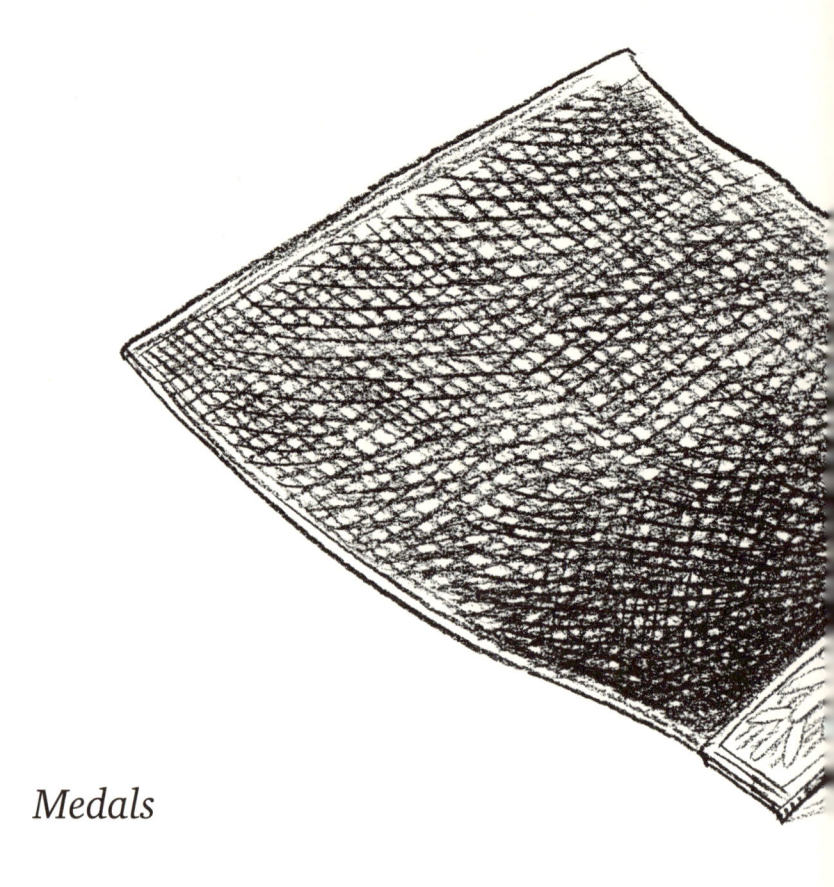

I won a competition.
They gave me a medal.
I wore it on my chest.

Mummy ran a marathon; came first place.
They gave her a medal.
She wore it round her neck.

Daddy was very brave.
They gave him a medal.
I wish he was here to wear it.

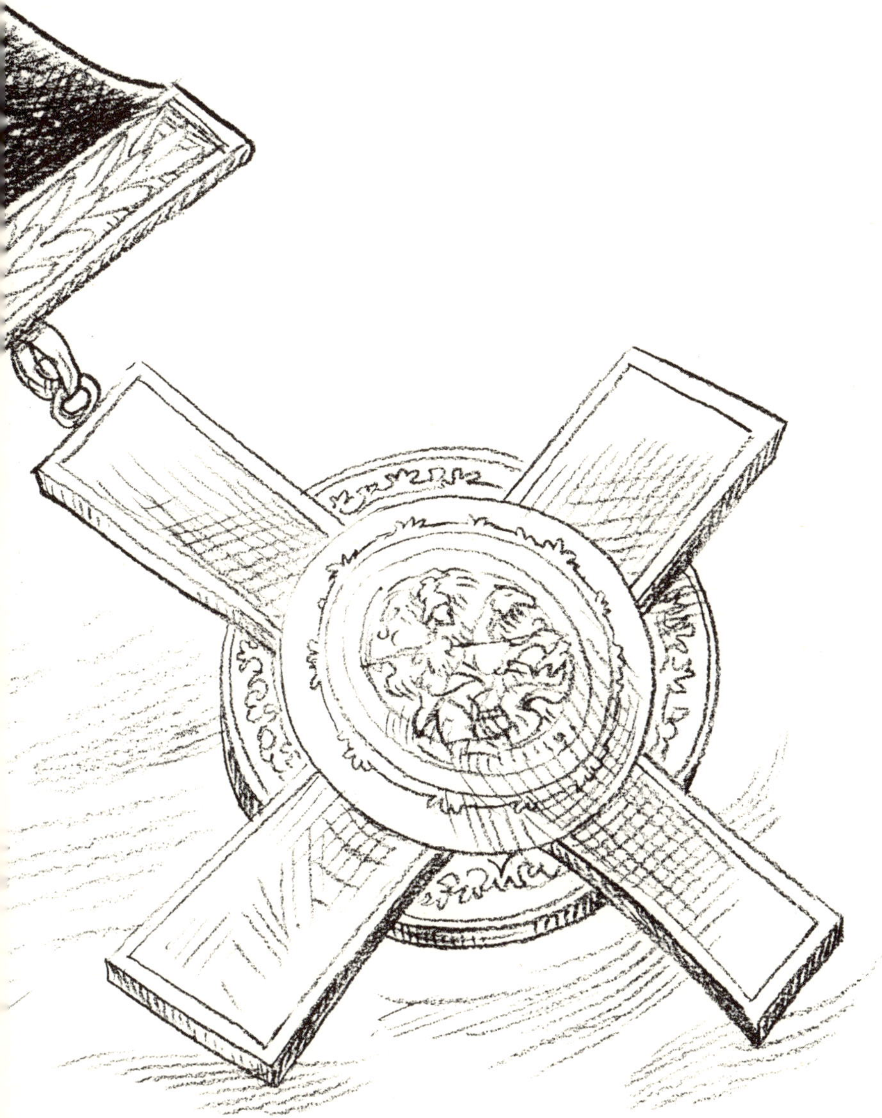

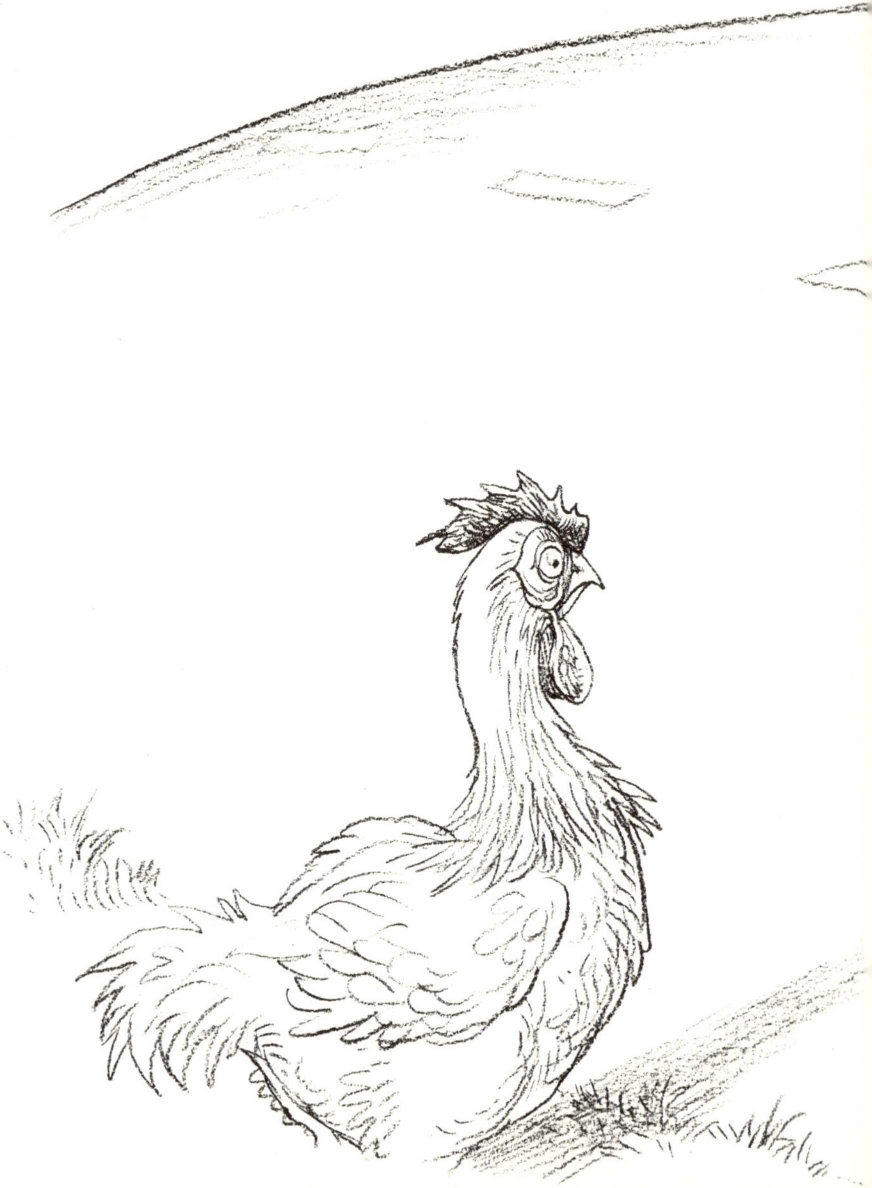

When the Chickens Crossed the Road

once, there was magic
when the chickens crossed the road
when the princess kissed the toad
when the poet wrote the ode
when the cracker broke the code

aye, once, there was magic
but the magic is no more
and now we need the chickens
like we never have before

Eulogy for Harry the Hedgehog

Harry the Hedgehog
wasn't a real hedgehog,
don't worry.

He was a stuffed, loved toy

that we left behind in a hotel room, all

alone.

It makes me sad just
to think of him, alone,
still, all these years later.

I remember saying to myself:

Goodbye, hedgehog.

Hello, young man.

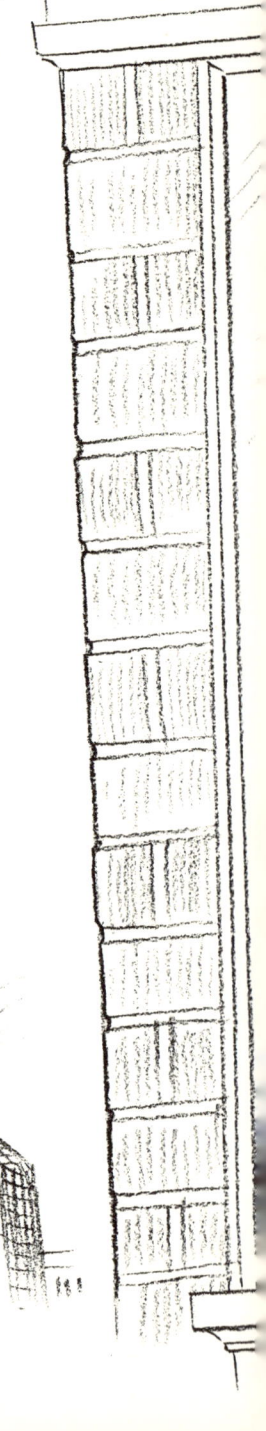

Untitled I: Paint on Canvas

Take a blank canvas and paint it black.
Let it dry, then fleck with white.
You have made the sky at night:
a cosmical backward dot-to-dot.
    Admire it.

Then, if you want, carve a moon,
carve a sun. Do whatever you like.
For this is your sky.
Create.
      Cause chaos.

The Arrogant Letter A

one day
the arrogant letter *A*
came up with a plan
to annihilate its fellow letters

it would butcher *B*
clobber *C*
leave *D* for dead
ultimately zapping *Z*

and then this world would start to sweat
lamenting the loss of its alphabet
forced to write
forever in fright: AAAAAAAAAAAAAAAA

AAAAA

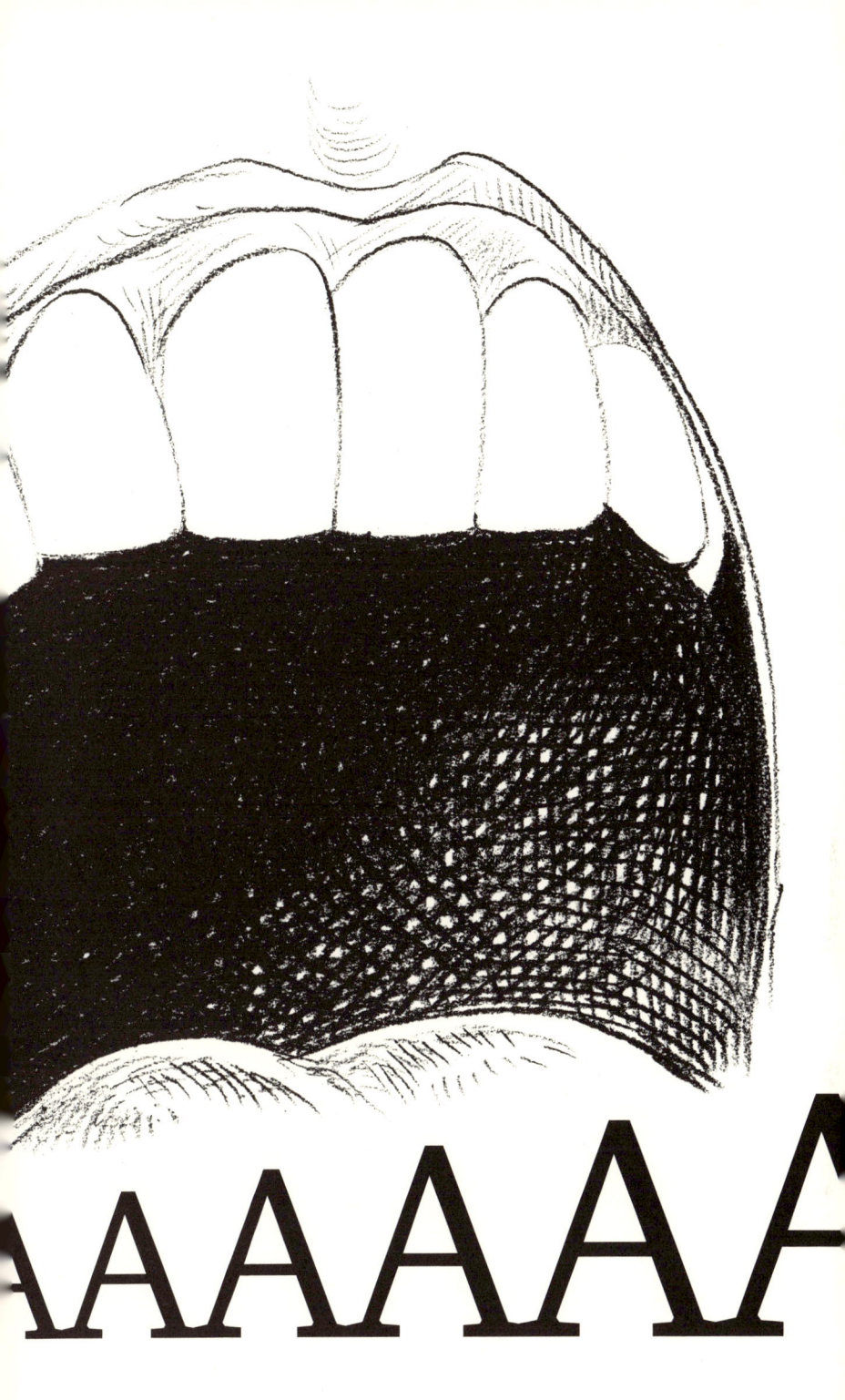

Garden Phantoms

Squirrels?!

Squirrels?!

Squirrels drive me nuts!

No ifs.
No ands.
No buts.

I hate the way they dig up grass.
They are a right pain in the garden.

Stealing food is awfully crass,
and they don't say please or pardon.

No ifs.
No ands.
No buts.

Squirrels drive me nuts!

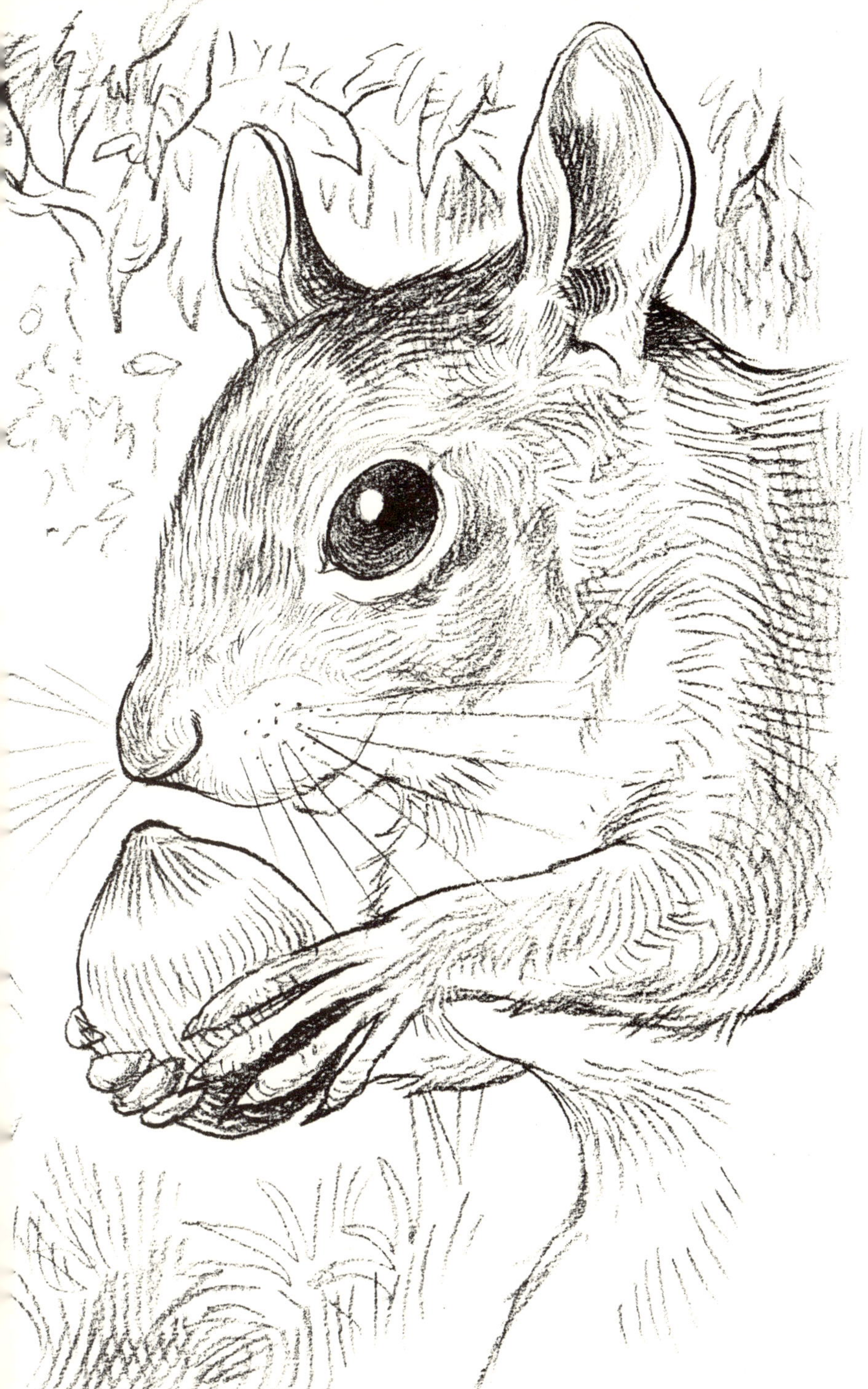

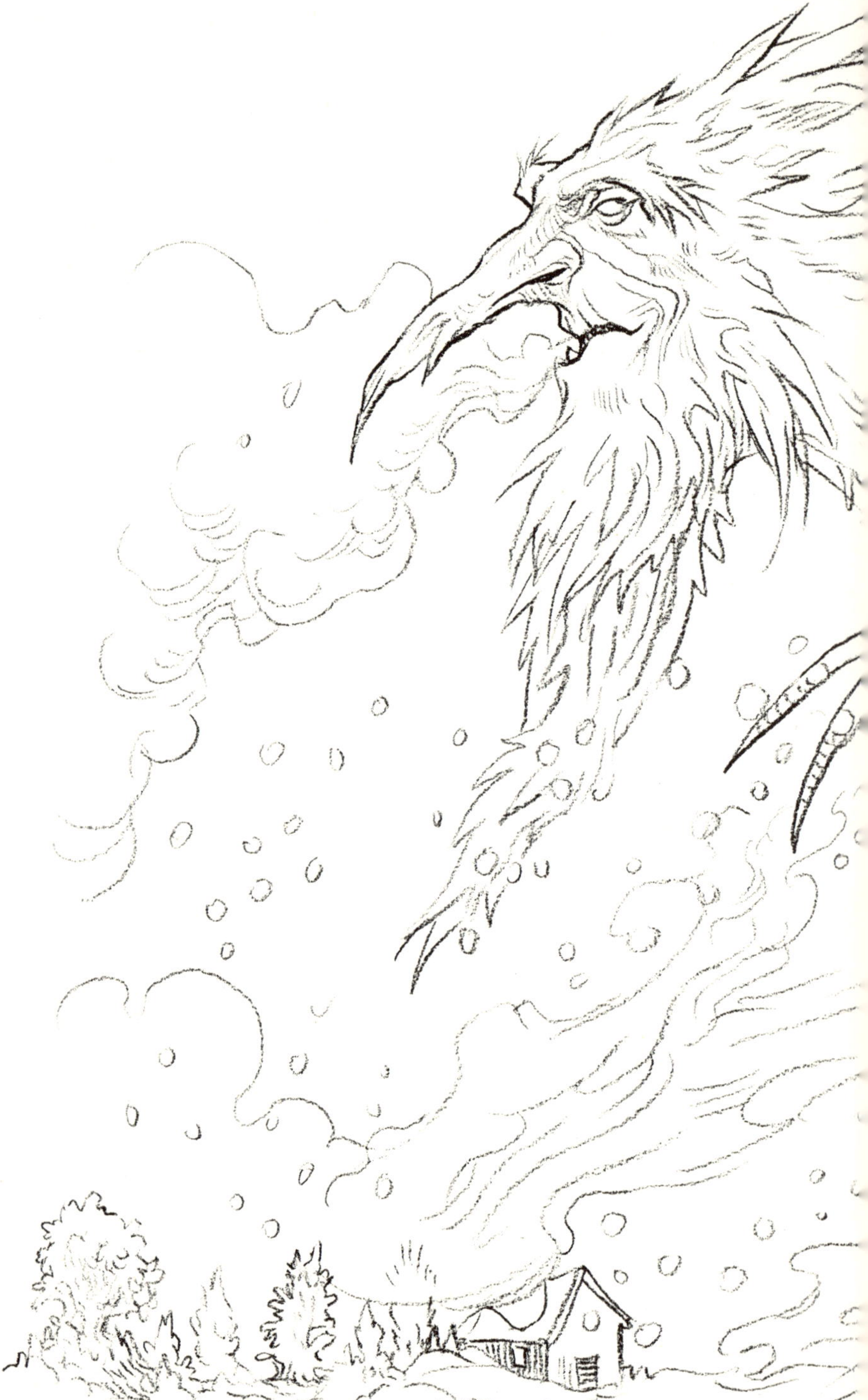

Welcome Winter

the leaves begin to crinkle
the fires turn to frost
the voice that sang of golden sand
now whispers winter's cost

farewell autumn, breathes the ice
knowing you's been awf'y nice

and with a feathered kiss of cold
snow: poetic rain
buries all the secrets
of old autumn's lost domain

The Rainbow in the Cupboard

we kept a rainbow
    at home
    in a cupboard
    tucked behind the pickles and peas

beautiful thing it was
    sparkled when we first saw it
    sparkled like you wouldn't believe

but we left it in the cupboard too long
    unloved
    and when we looked again
    all we found
    was rain

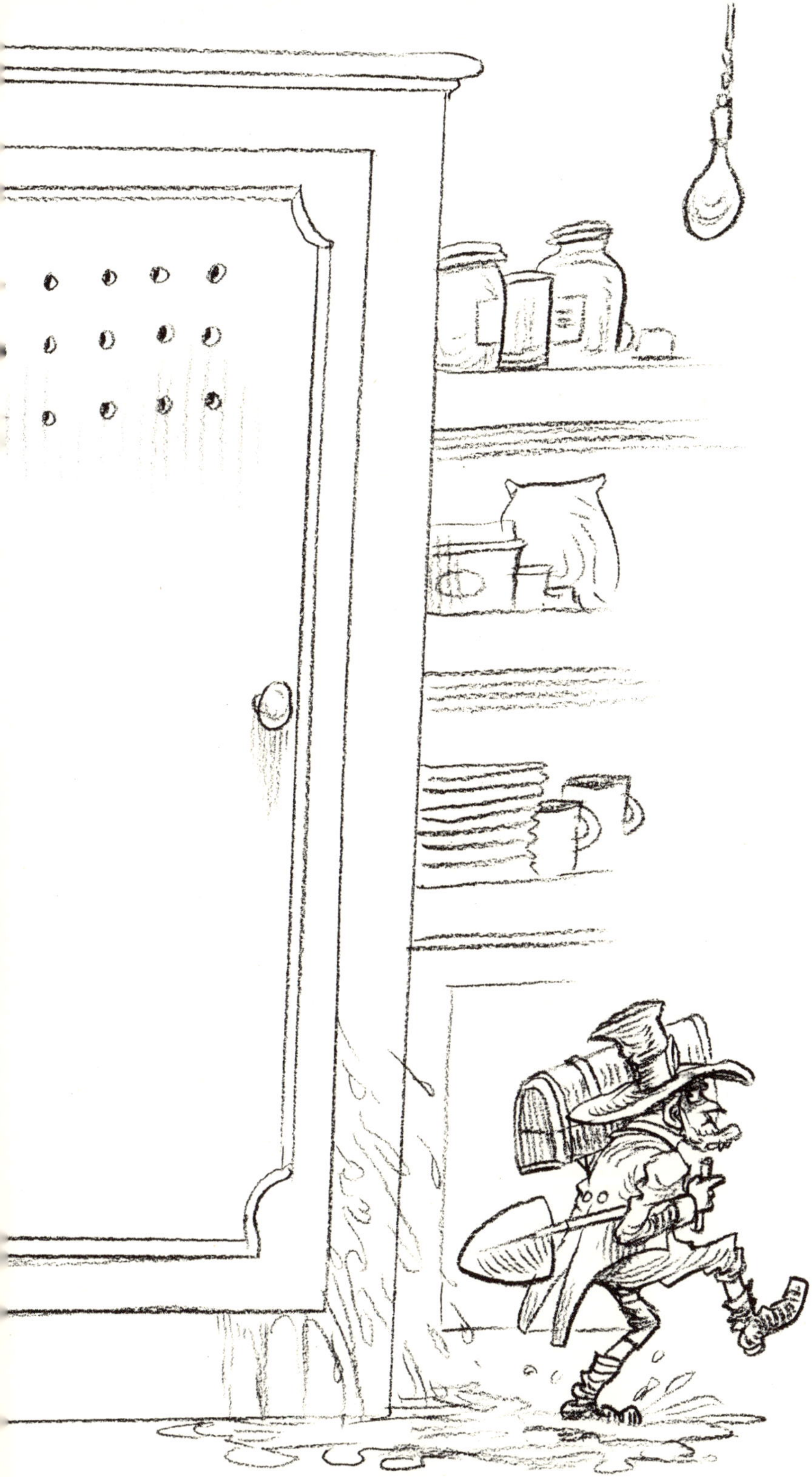

On Breakers

the sea salt supper
of a summer bruise
is swelled again //

the faraway dam
on a long ago beach
is set to rebuckle //

the lost spade
last seen by crumbled castle
is washed ashore on breakers //

the seagull's cry
shrills the sky anew //

Rejoice! Rejoice! //

    —the boats are coming home.

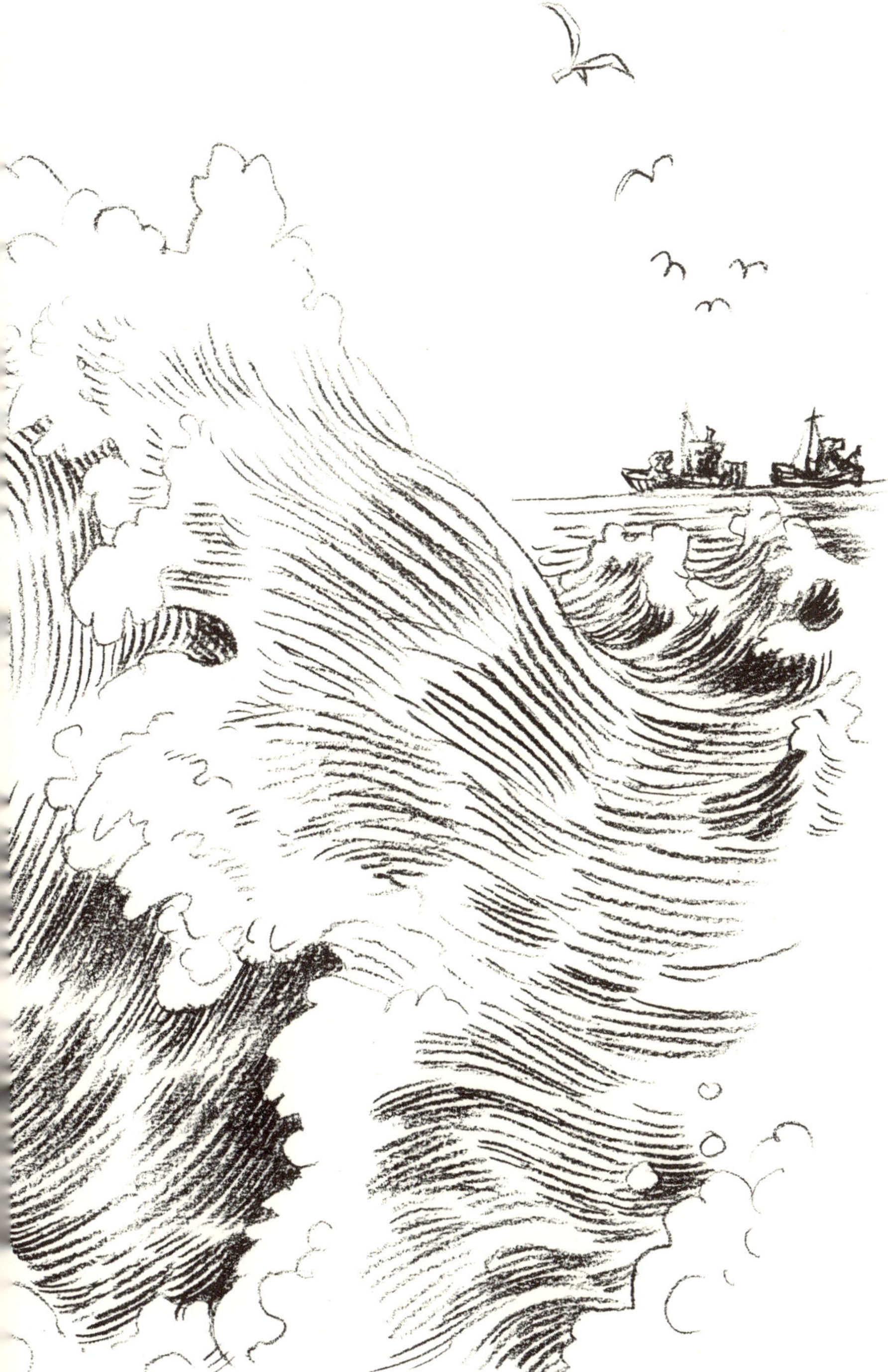

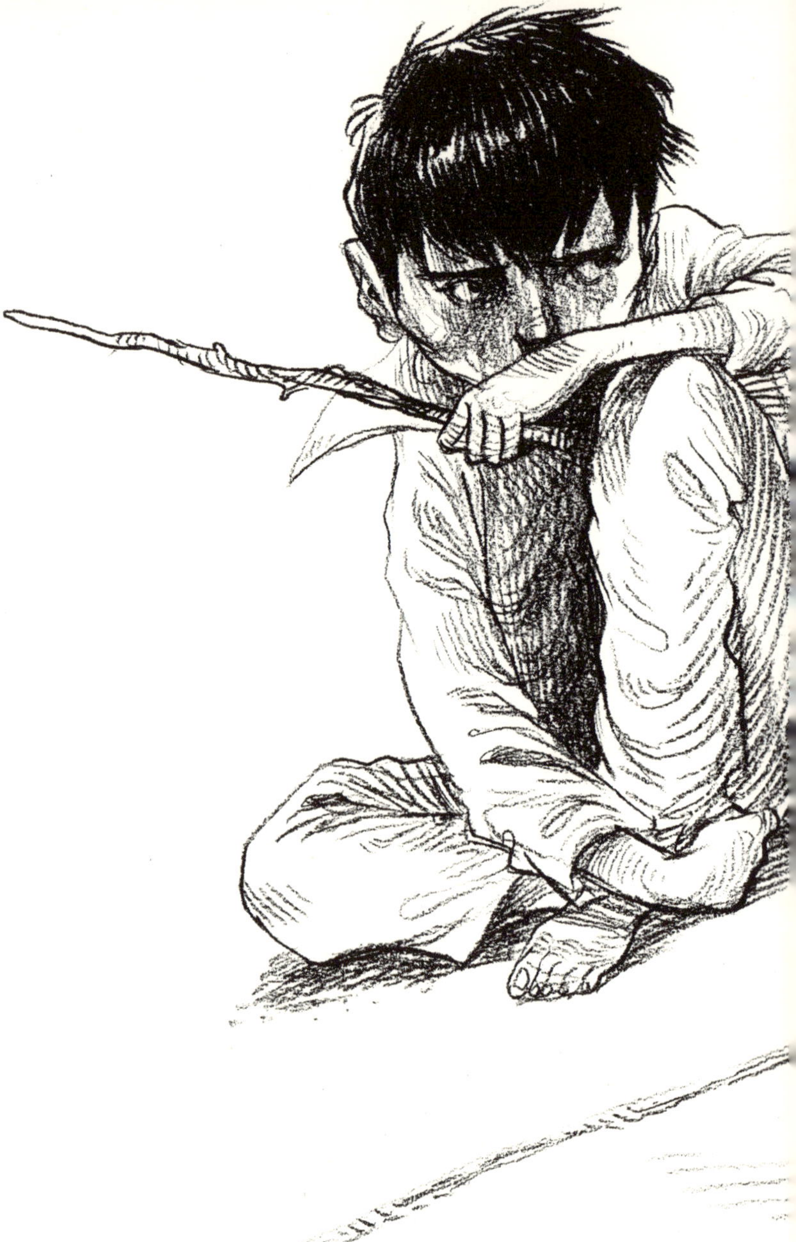

A Line in the Sand

Here,
take this stick,
this simple stick,
and draw a line in the sand.

Good. Good.
This is your line, not mine,
and now you have a choice:

step over the line; or,
let the sea consume it,
the tide take it away.

Remember.

Your line. Your life. Your choice.

Happy New Year

Happy New Laughter
Happy New Smiles
Happy New Moments
Happy New Miles
Happy New Journey
Happy New Look
Happy New Chapter
Happy New Book
Happy New Challenge
Happy New Chance
Happy New Song
Happy New Dance
Happy New Candle and
Happy New Cheer
Happy New Happy and
Happy New Year

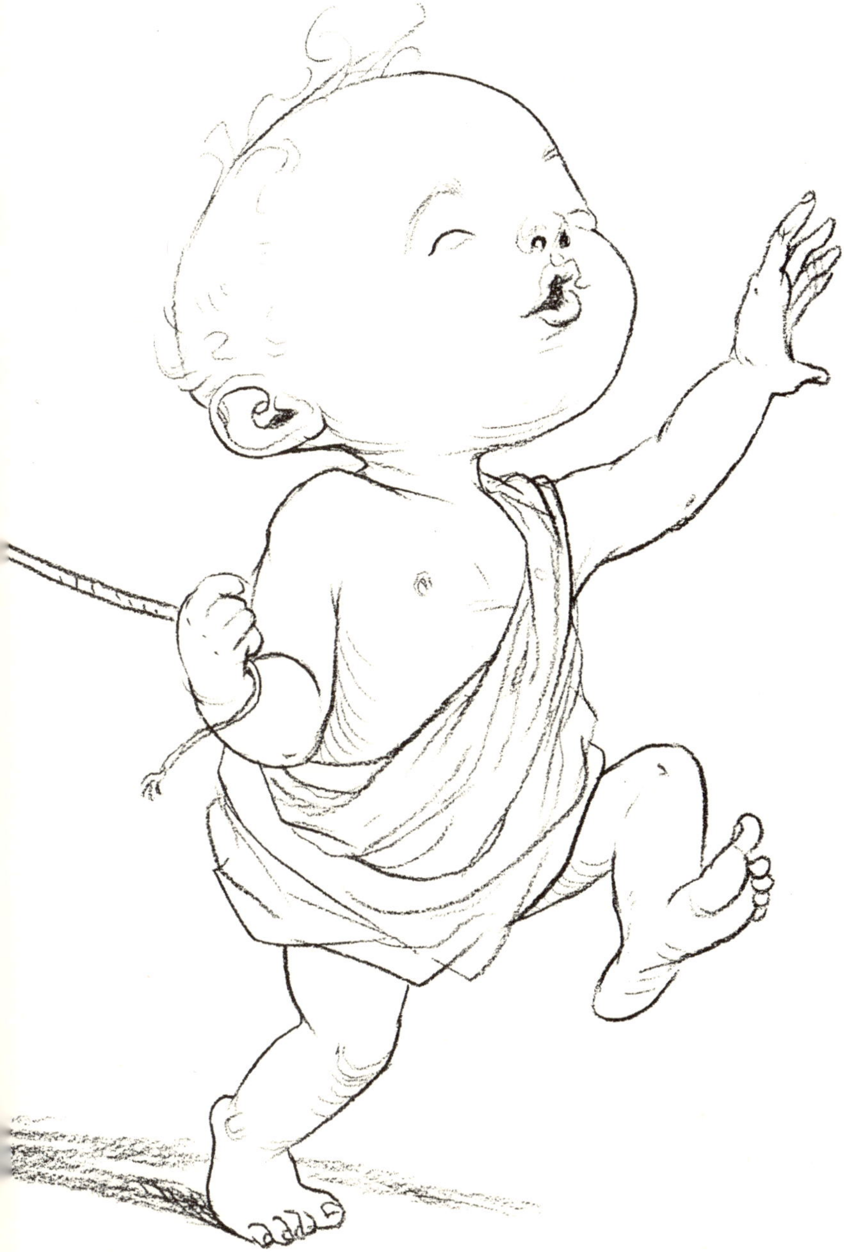

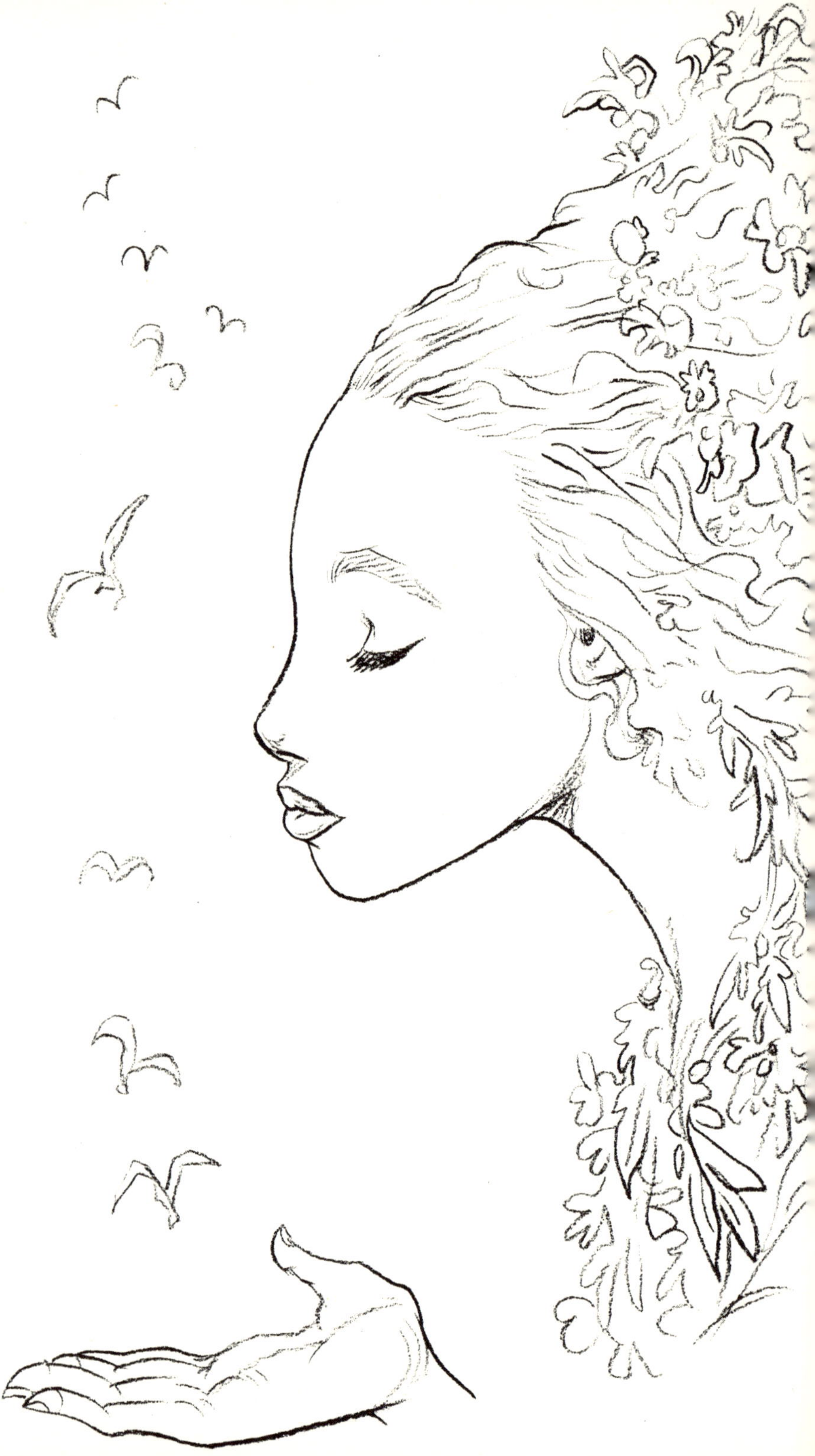

Still Earth

Stillness.

Earth holding breath.

The sky, a brilliance of blue,

its blush like newly polished brass.

The air, clean and sweet,

unsung by lips:

a language locked away.

No wind today.

Just stillness.

Stillness.

Just air and light and calm and earth.

And in the absence of the words:

birds.

What We Wear

Look! Look!
Do you like my dress?

> No, no,
> I confess.

Look! Look!
Do you like my shoes?

> No, no,
> they simply amuse.

Look! Look!
Do you like my ring?

> No, no,
> obnoxious bling.

Look! Look!
Do you like my 'do?

> No, no,
> I just like you for being *you*.

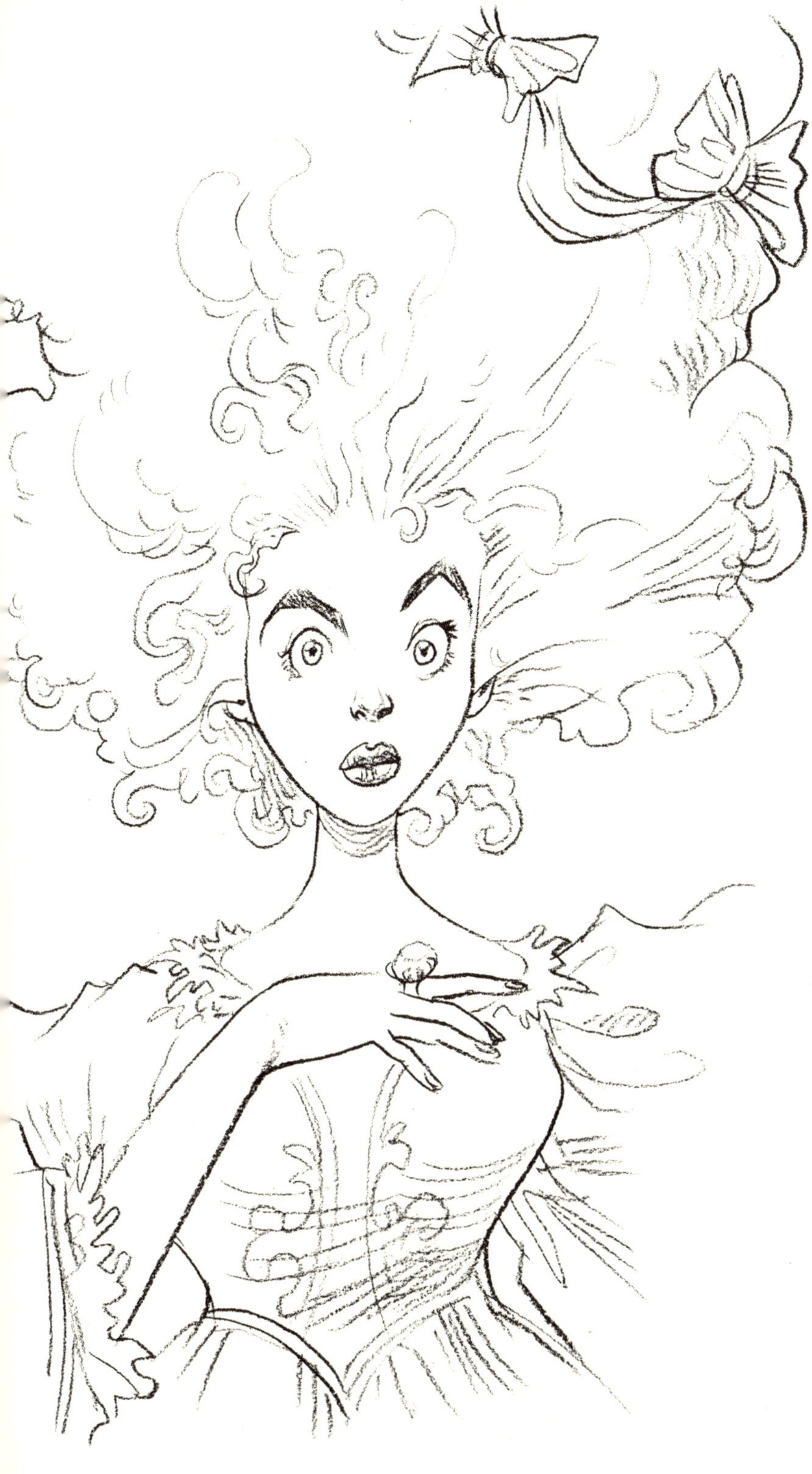

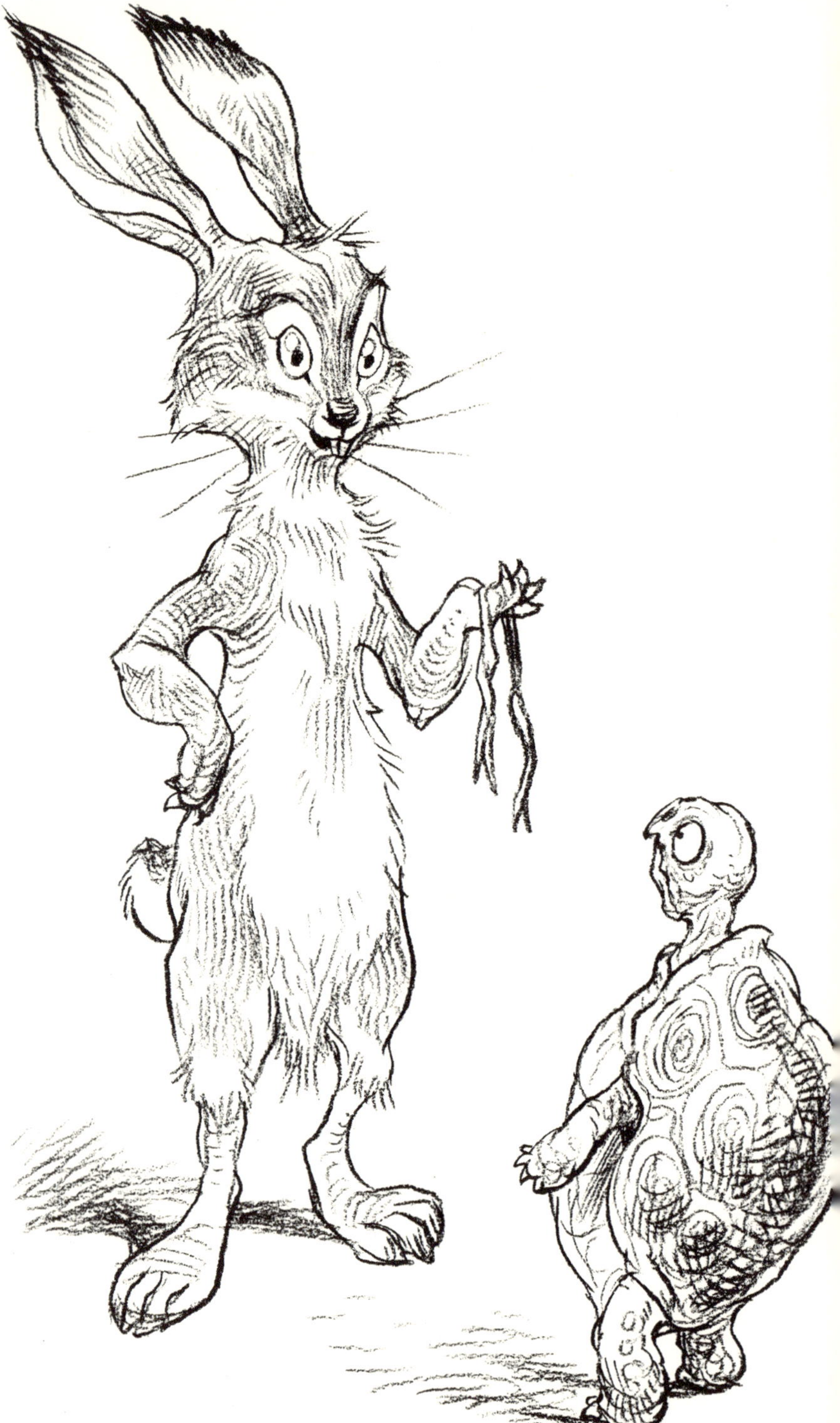

The Three-Legged Race

I want to run a race with you,
        three-legged, joined at the hip,
and if we trip, we'll fall together.

Land   in a tumble   of awkward
   limbs   and laugh,   support
     each other's strength to stand
                and re-centre ourselves,
             ready to rejoin the race.

    Our pace:

           Step

Together

           Step

Together

           Step

Golden Retrieval

give me the ball

give me the ball

give me the ball

please

give me the YES! RUN! RUN! RUN! RUN!
run! you can have the ball RUN!
run! RUN!
run! give me the ball RUN!
run! RUN!
run! give me the ball RUN!
run! RUN!
run! give me the ball RUN!
run! please RUN!
run! RUN!
run! GRRRHHGHRRGHHH!!! run!

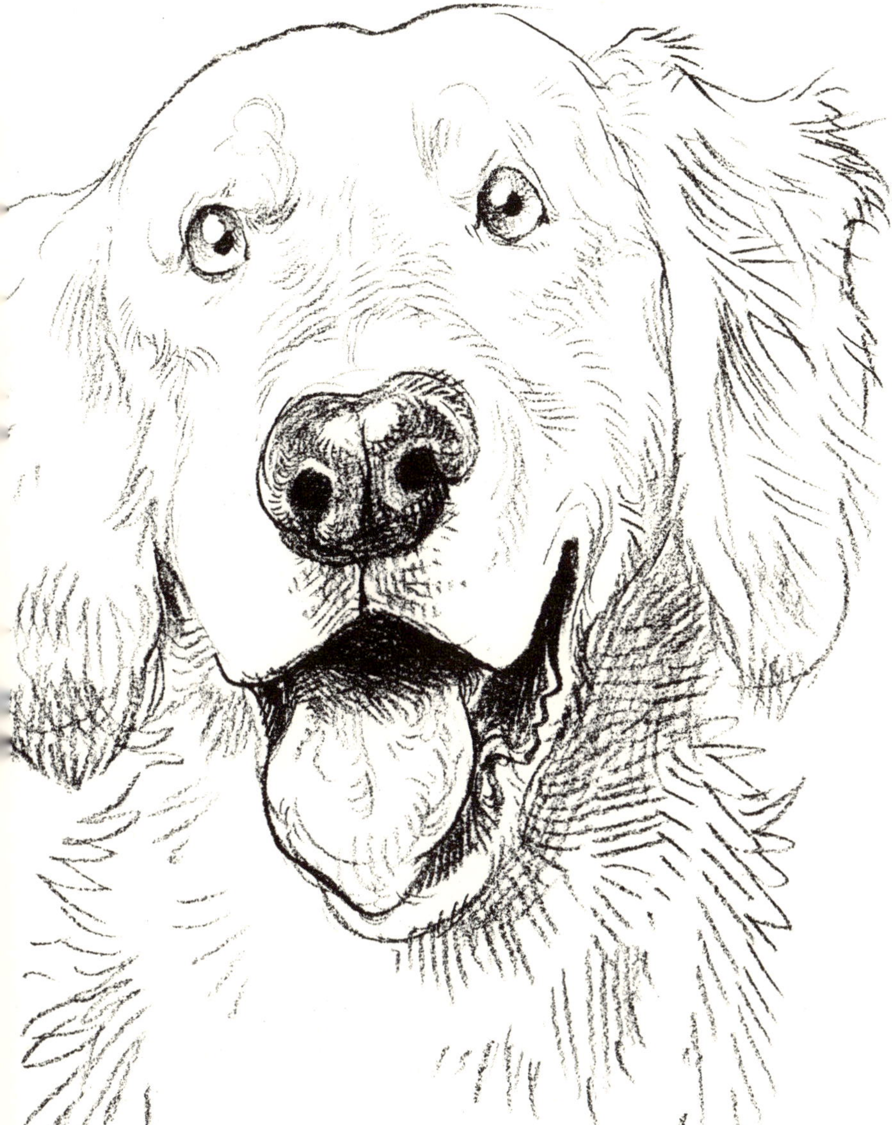

Tales from a Garden

Bees buzz deliriously
flower to flower.
Butterflies flutter
by blade, by blade.
The hedgerows hum
with wildfire song.
Worms chorus line
their soil theatre.
Dragonflies slide
on sunbeams
as sunflowers
stretch skyward
amid a hopscotch
of ants.

A single magpie lands.

Time to move on.

This is not my garden.

Two Slugs Just Chilling in the Compost Bin

Brian?

Dave?

What you doing, Brian?

Chomping on my orange peel.

Cool.

Dave?

Brian?

What you doing, Dave?

Snoozing in the lid.

Cool.

Brian?

Dave?

Aaaaaaaaaah! Daylight!

Daylight! Aaaaaaaaaah!

Make it stop! Make it—

Oh. Thank goodness.

That was too much.

Dave?

Dave?

You up there, Dave?

Ooooooo! Fresh grub.

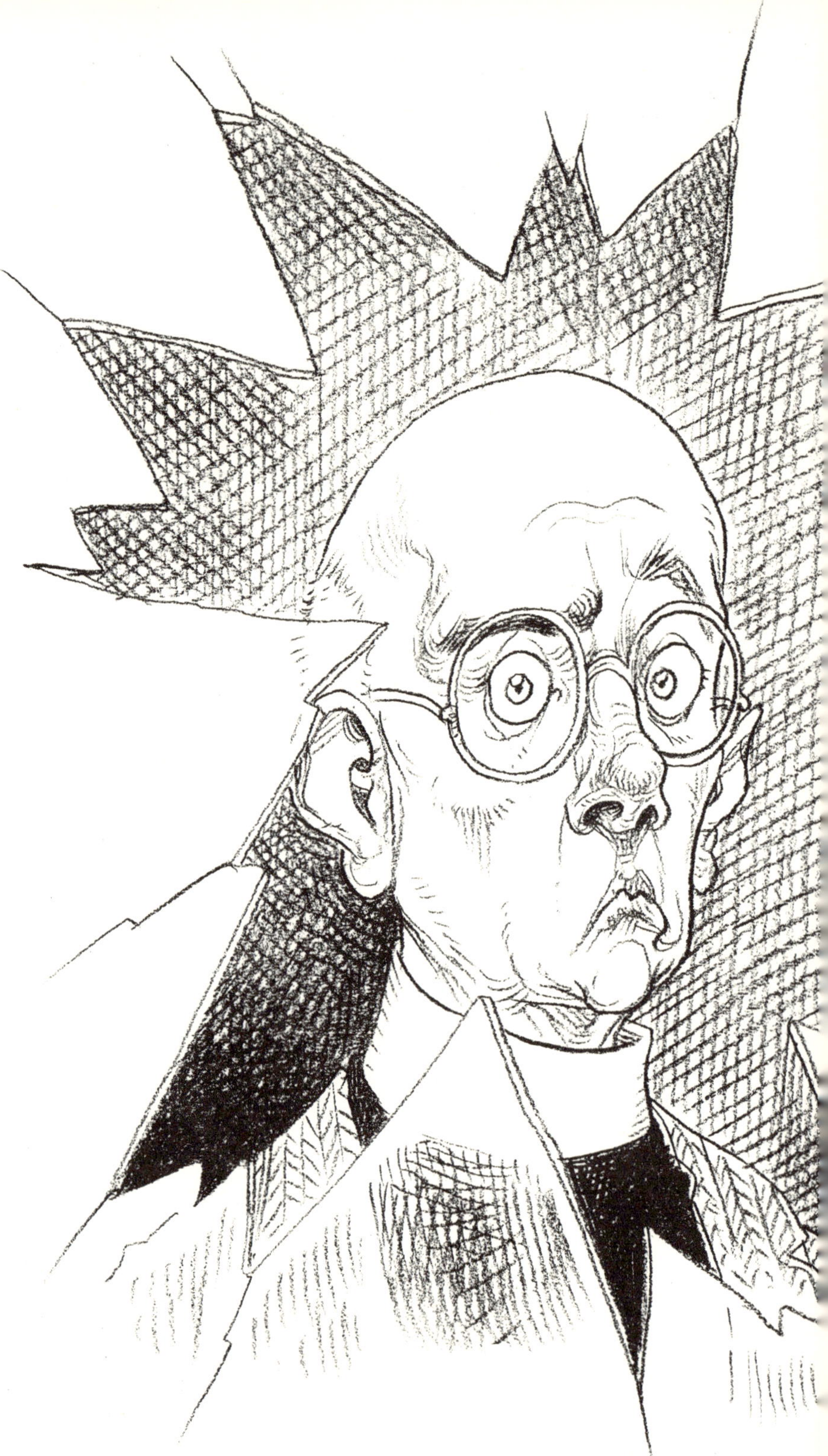

An Incident in Kingston Hall

Yesterday, in Kingston Hall,
I found a weathered cricket ball
surrounded by some shards of glass
and a tiny tuft of grass.

Of course I knew which rascal threw it;
there's only one round here who'd do it.
So I returned the ball, it's true,
through *his* window. Wouldn't you?

Murder Mystery

Bang!

    The doctor — dead.

Bang!

    The professor — dead.

Bang!

    The reverend — dead.

        "I will find the culprit soon,"
        the detective gravely said.

Bang!

    The housemaid — dead.

Bang!

    The butler — dead.

        "The identity of the murderer,
        I'm glad to say I know it!"

Bang!

    The detective — dead,

        murdered . . . . . by the poet.

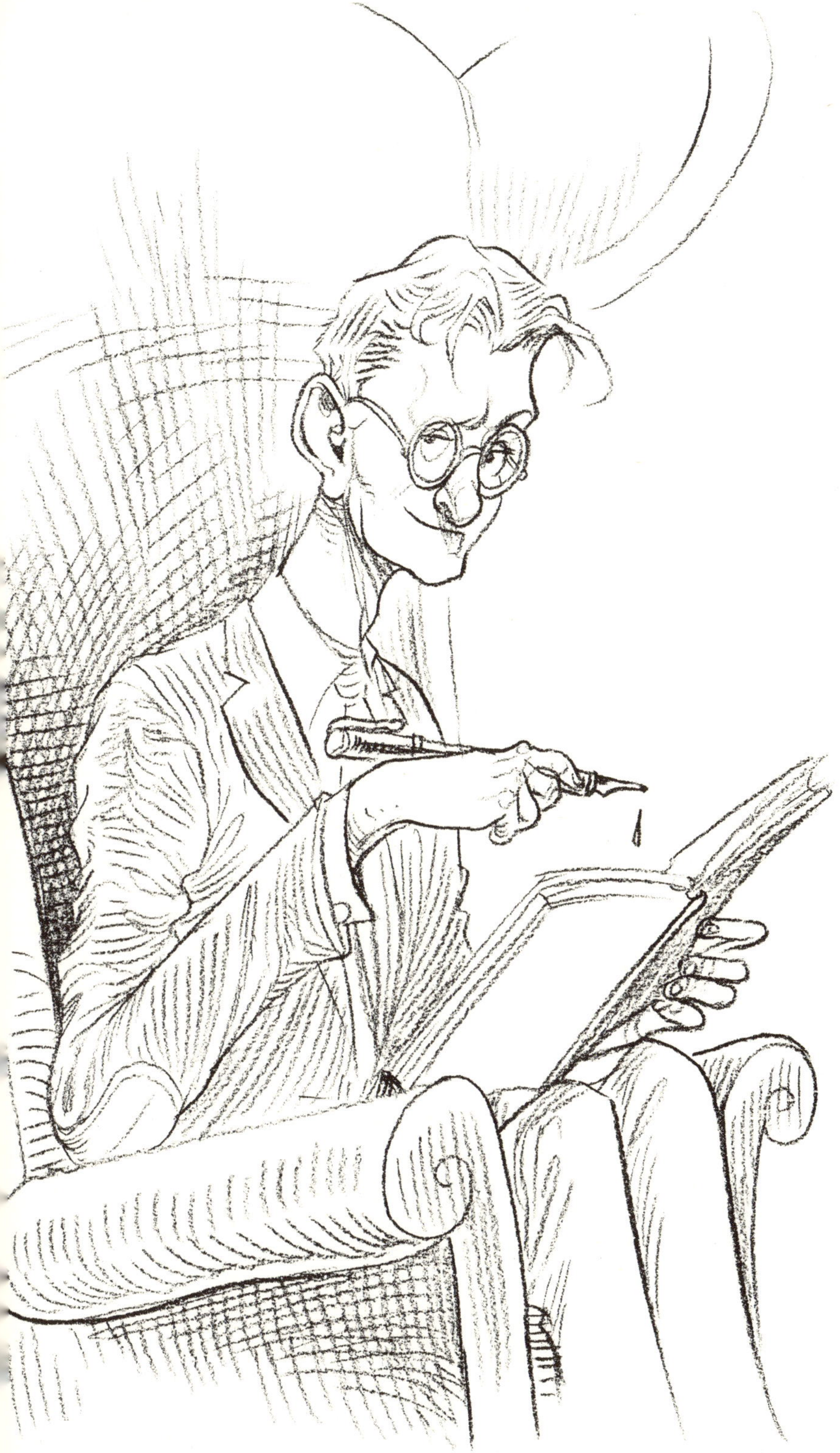

You Make Me So ACROSTIC

Acrostic poetry, to some, is fine
Concealing a word along its spine
Really easy to teach but often contrived
Obscuring ideas that could have easily thrived
Stoppering such imagination
The schools are rife with acrostic contamination
I will never write this type of verse
See, to me, there's nothing worse

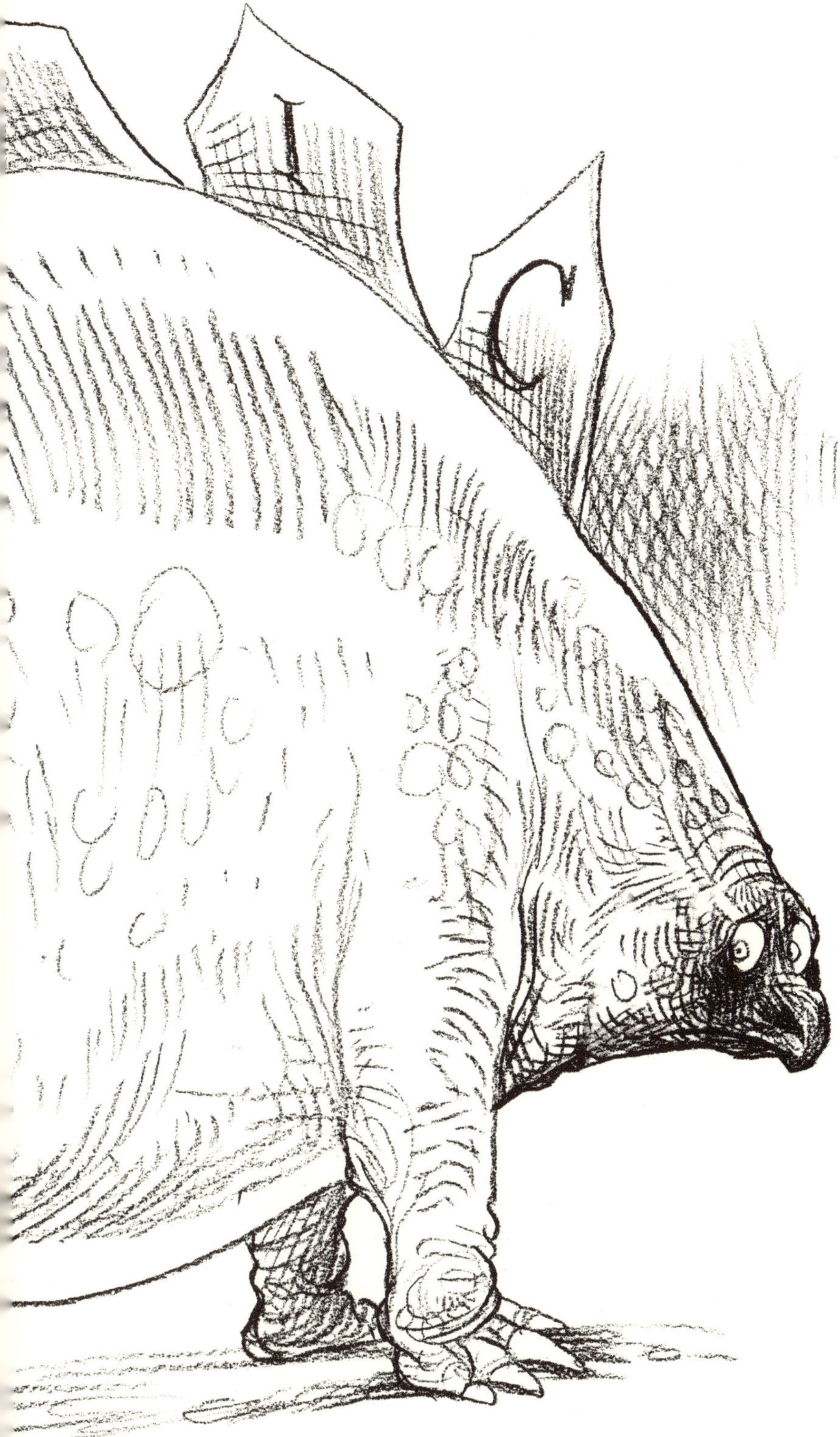
I
C

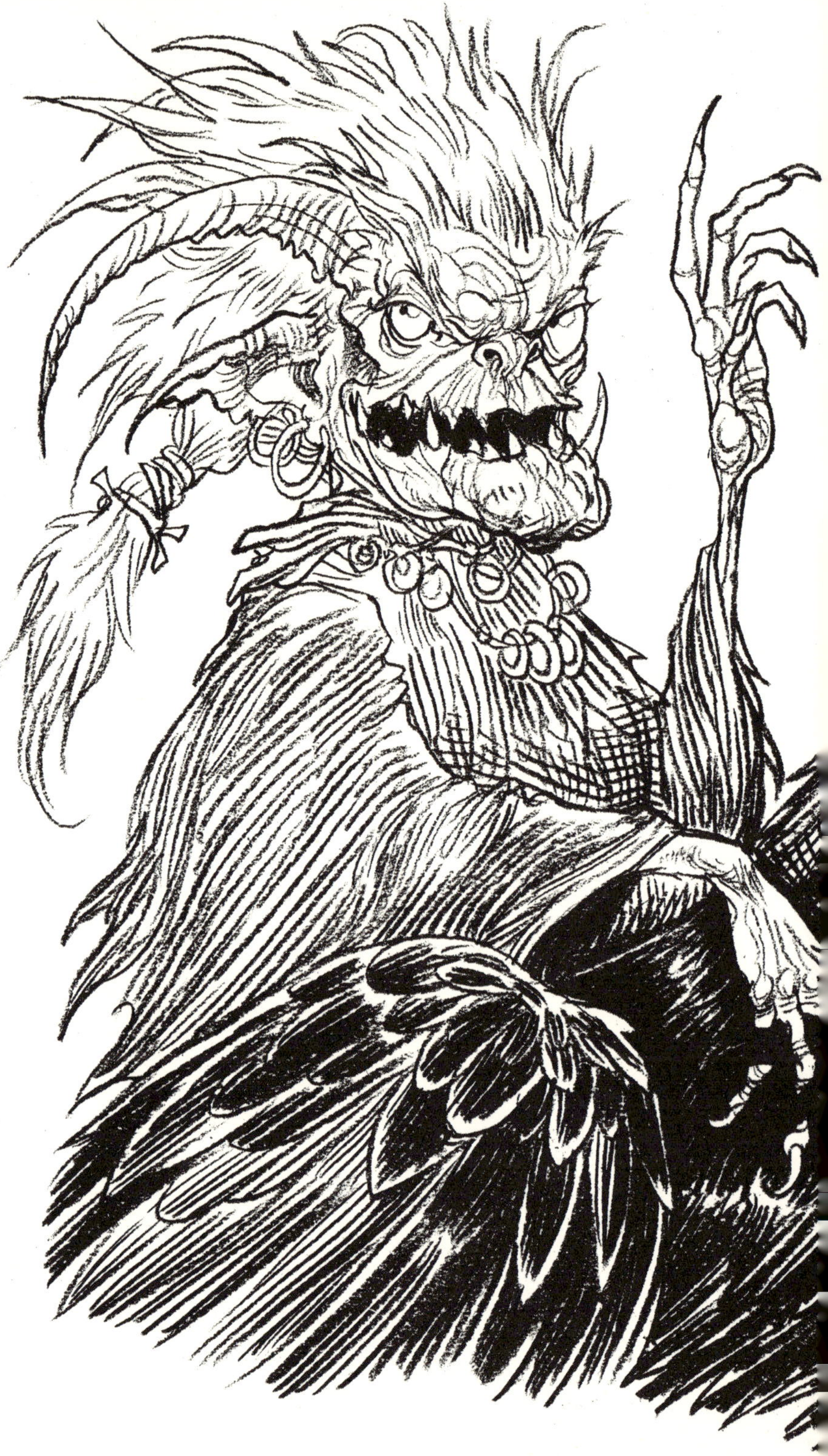

Apocalyptic Scene from an Otherwise Unwritten Story

——————————] then Chevious, the imp of green hair and tricksy truths, laced its fingers through the feathers of the Last Raven. *Time to bid this dying world farewell*, thought Cheevy, taking in the viridescent sky and the still smoking remains of the once great Forest. Vaingloriously, they took flight and flew [——————

Advice on How to Care for a Fallen Star

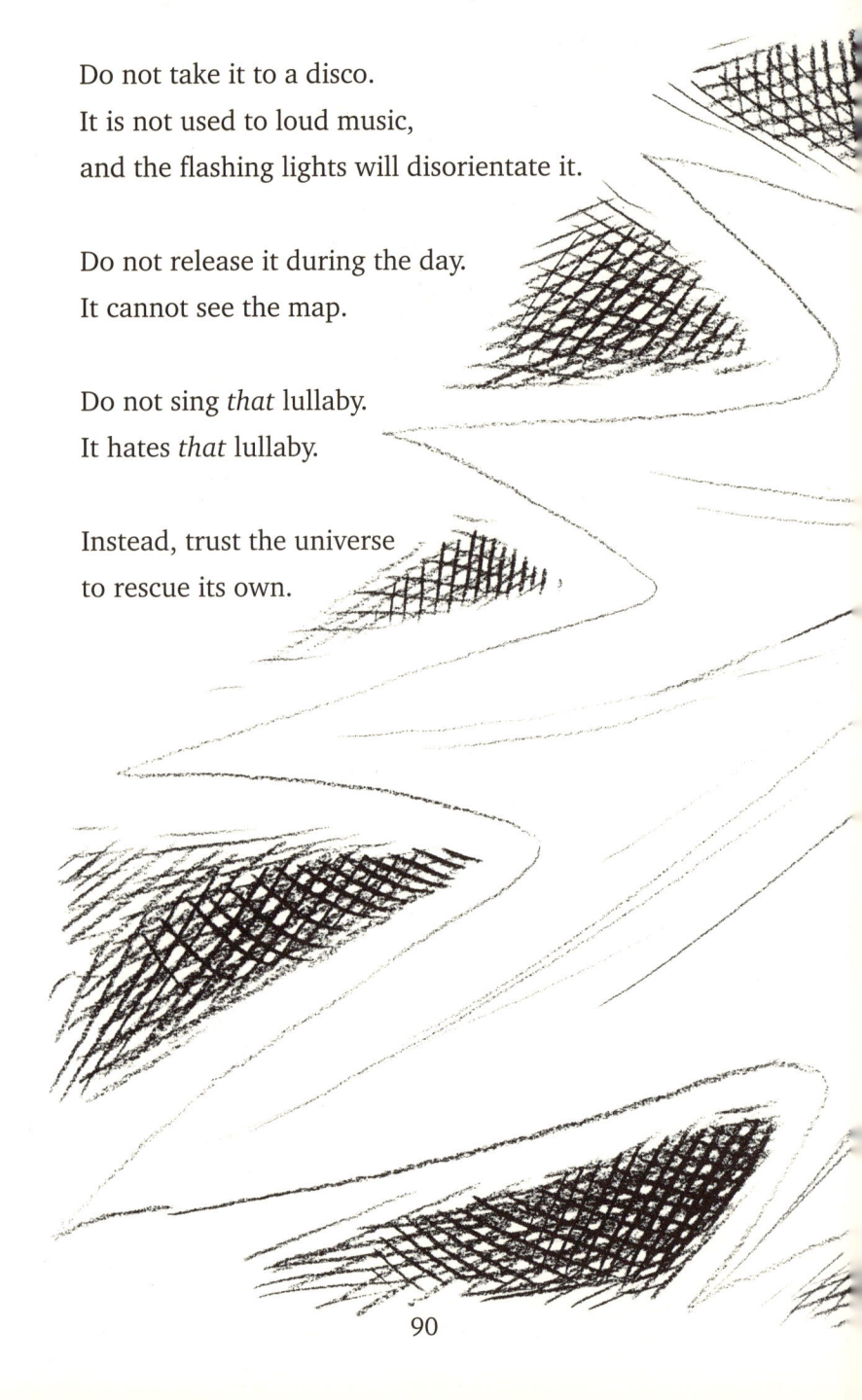

Do not take it to a disco.
It is not used to loud music,
and the flashing lights will disorientate it.

Do not release it during the day.
It cannot see the map.

Do not sing *that* lullaby.
It hates *that* lullaby.

Instead, trust the universe
to rescue its own.

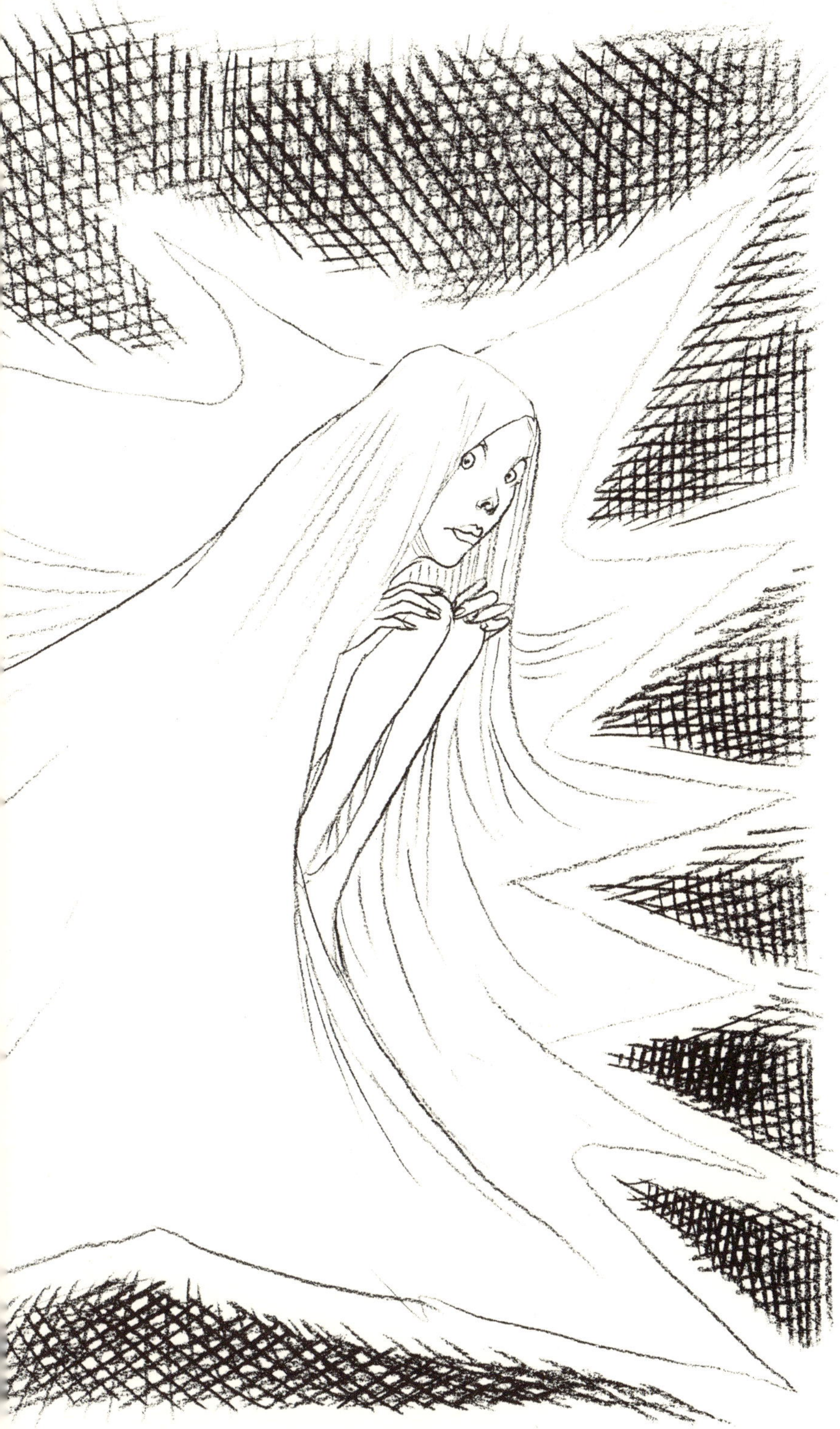

Return of the Dwellers

and they came

>crawling from the caves
>>and the ponds
>>>and the places of dark

>>>>limb over limb

>harsh brilliant light
>>>>like daggers in their eyes

they came

        clay crumbling from their skin

                their cracking bones
            the birdsong of a newborn age

they came
        and they came

                and they come

They Built a Bridge

How do you build a bridge?
> asked the boy.

With my help,
> replied his shadow.

> Together, they built a bridge.

How do you cross a bridge?
> asked the boy.

Hand in hand,
> replied his shadow.

> They crossed.

How do you burn a bridge?
> asked the boy.

Alone,
> replied his shadow.

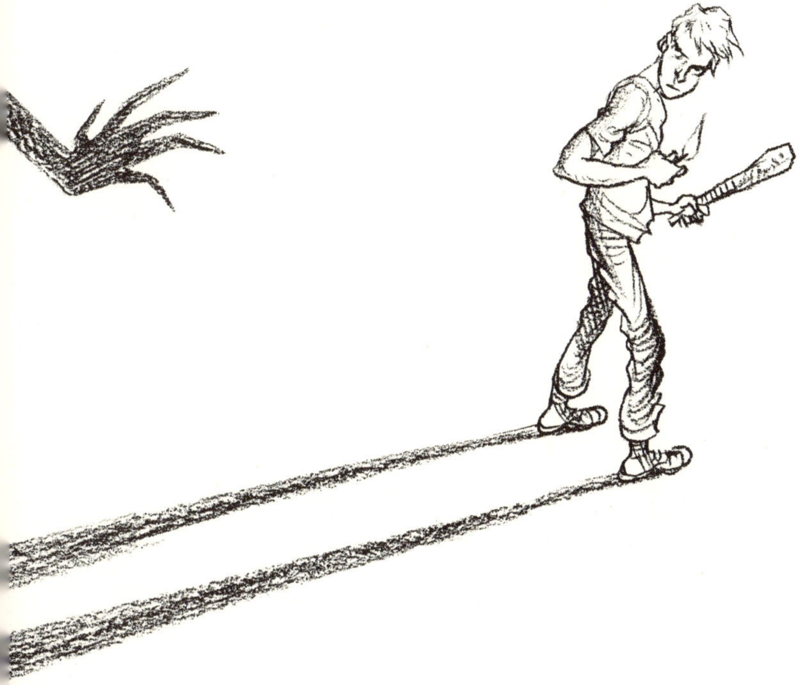

The Sun's Lament

Sunset.

The Sun looks at Planet Earth
despondently
and sighs
a heavy
sigh.

Will they ever learn?

Then, as at the end
of every other First Day,
the Sun gently bends the universe,
polishes up its most hopeful beams,
and smiles its most promising smile.

Here we go again . . . . .

Sunrise.

Nine Lives of Cat

my first was dawn
start of the tale

my second, shale
shoreline echo

my third, meadow
evergreen giver

my fourth, river
cool and calm

my fifth, farm
clatter of cattle

my sixth, castle
royal kitty

my seventh, city
smoky and sweaty

my eighth, confetti
taking a bow

my ninth, now

Life on the Rock

There's hope within a hermit crab
patiently waiting in the vacancy chain
for its new home, a passing on of shells.
It pays for each crab to care for each shell
that they carry, knowing they'll inherit other
shells from other crabs, just like them: sharing
                                    life on the rock.

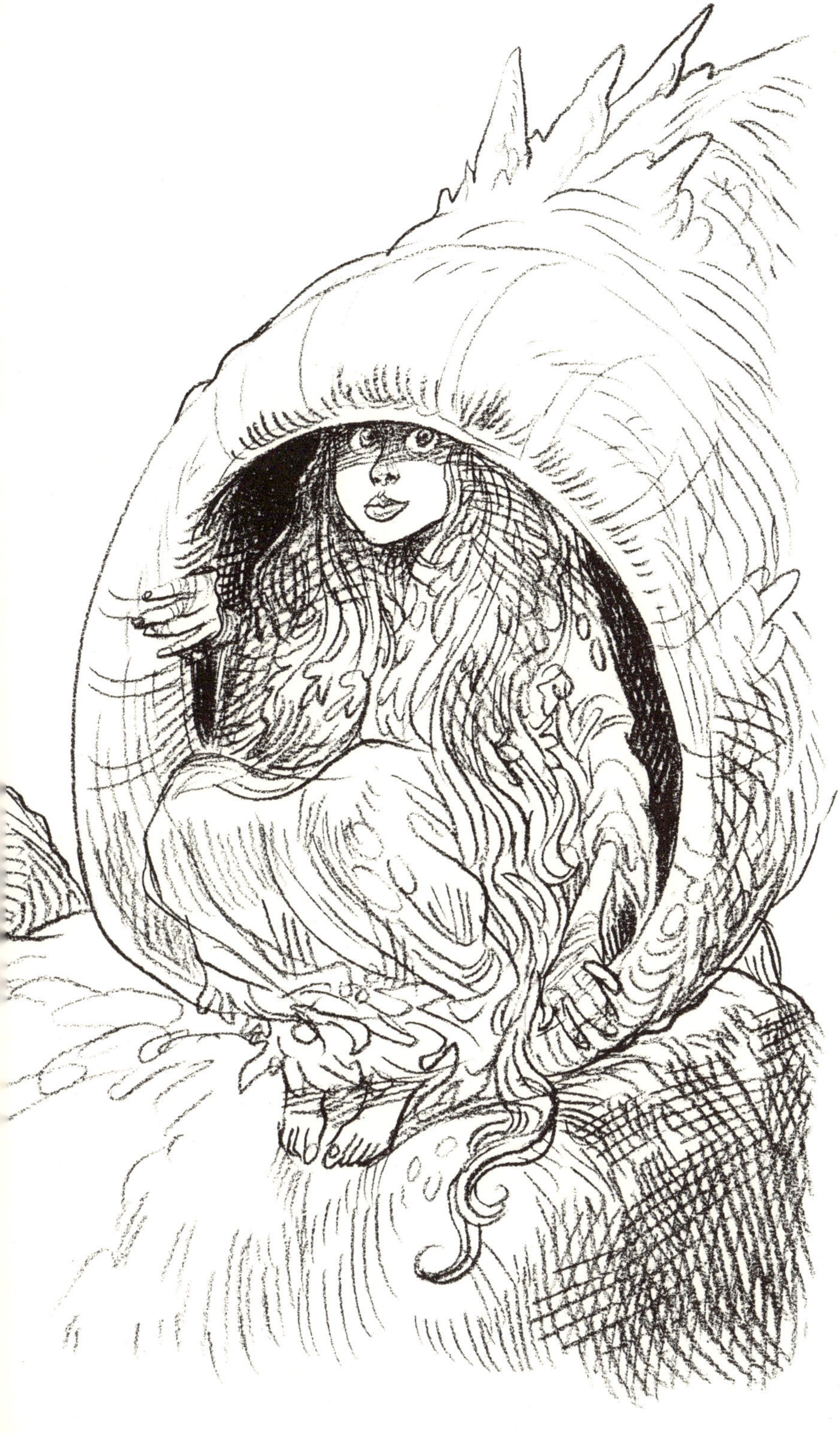

The Boys at Summer's End

At summer's end,
we rode our bikes to the edge of the city,
eking out the last of the sun.

We reminisced and lit a fire in a rusted metal drum,
a last little light before the dark of the wild beyond.

Only the night train knew of our den.

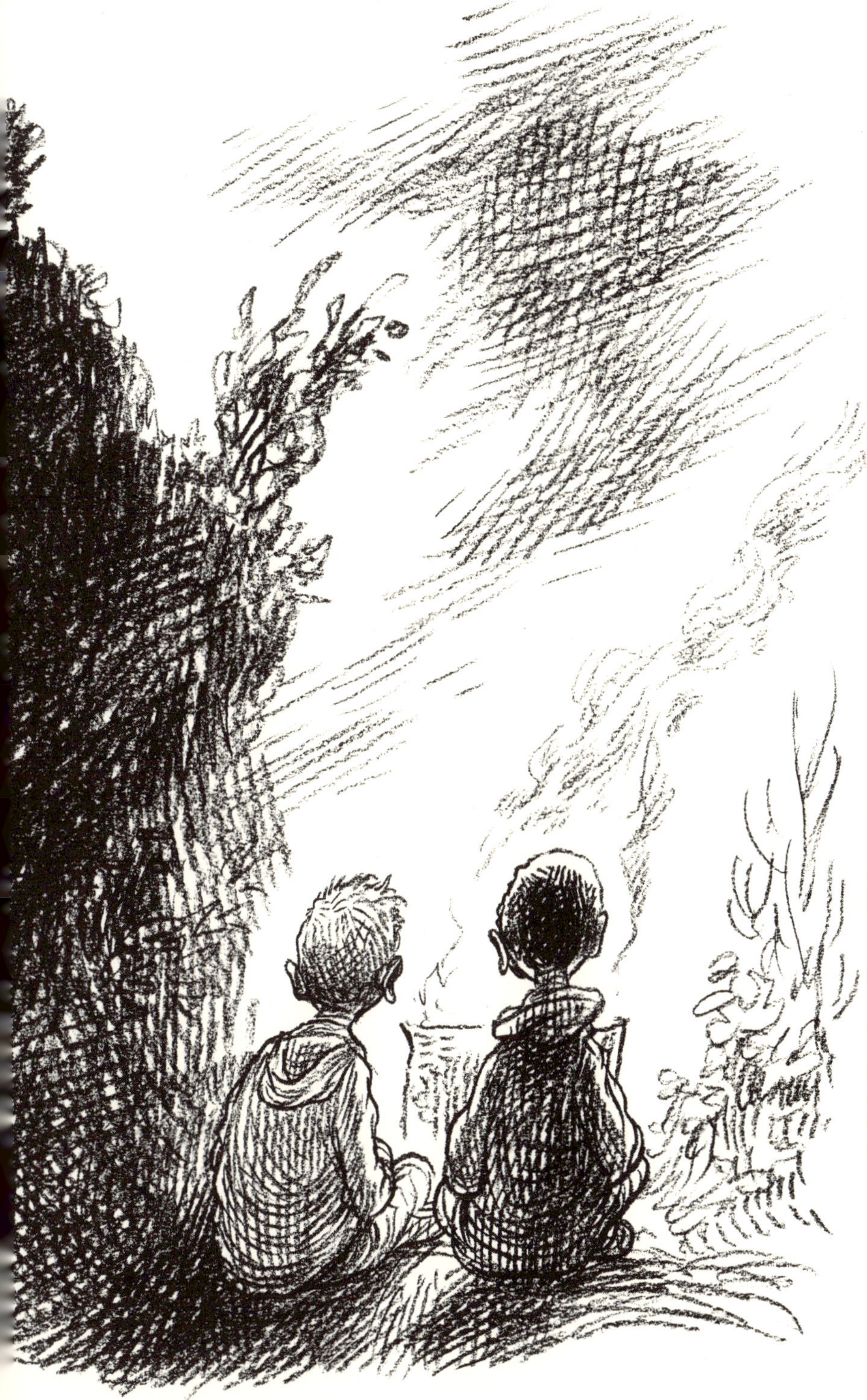

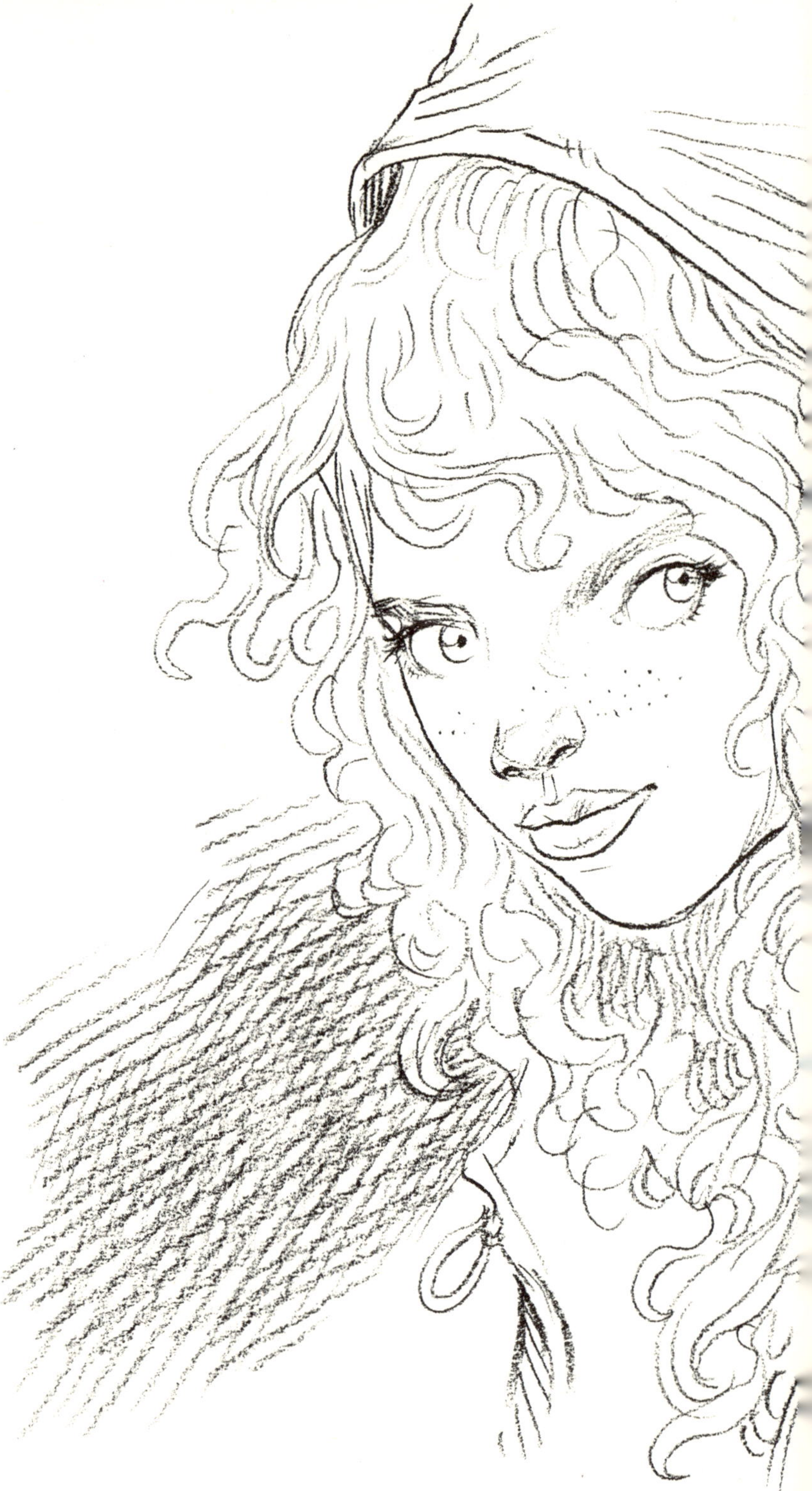

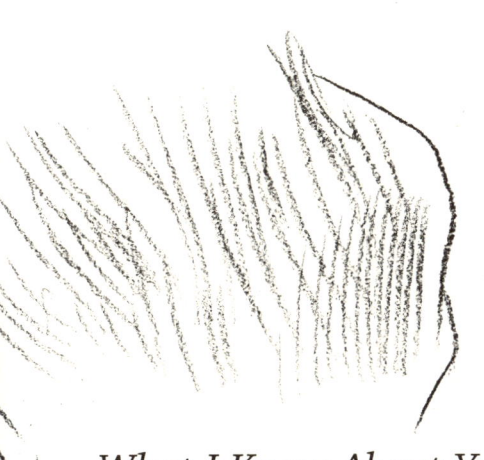

What I Know About You

You are a dazzling human, unique:
a soup of swirling starlight wrapped in skin.

You, a tidy mess of contradictions:
sometimes spark; sometimes flame.

You are storms and teapots and crinkled crunchy leaves.
You are beginnings and endings and all the in-betweens.

Yes, I am going to know you forever.

Snow Globes

The path upstairs was lined with snow globes,
each a little capturing of a moment, a memory.

In passing, each was for the tilting of a miniature world,
a shaking up of old snow, sent sifting through new light.

Now, I make my own snow globes
and call them *poems*.

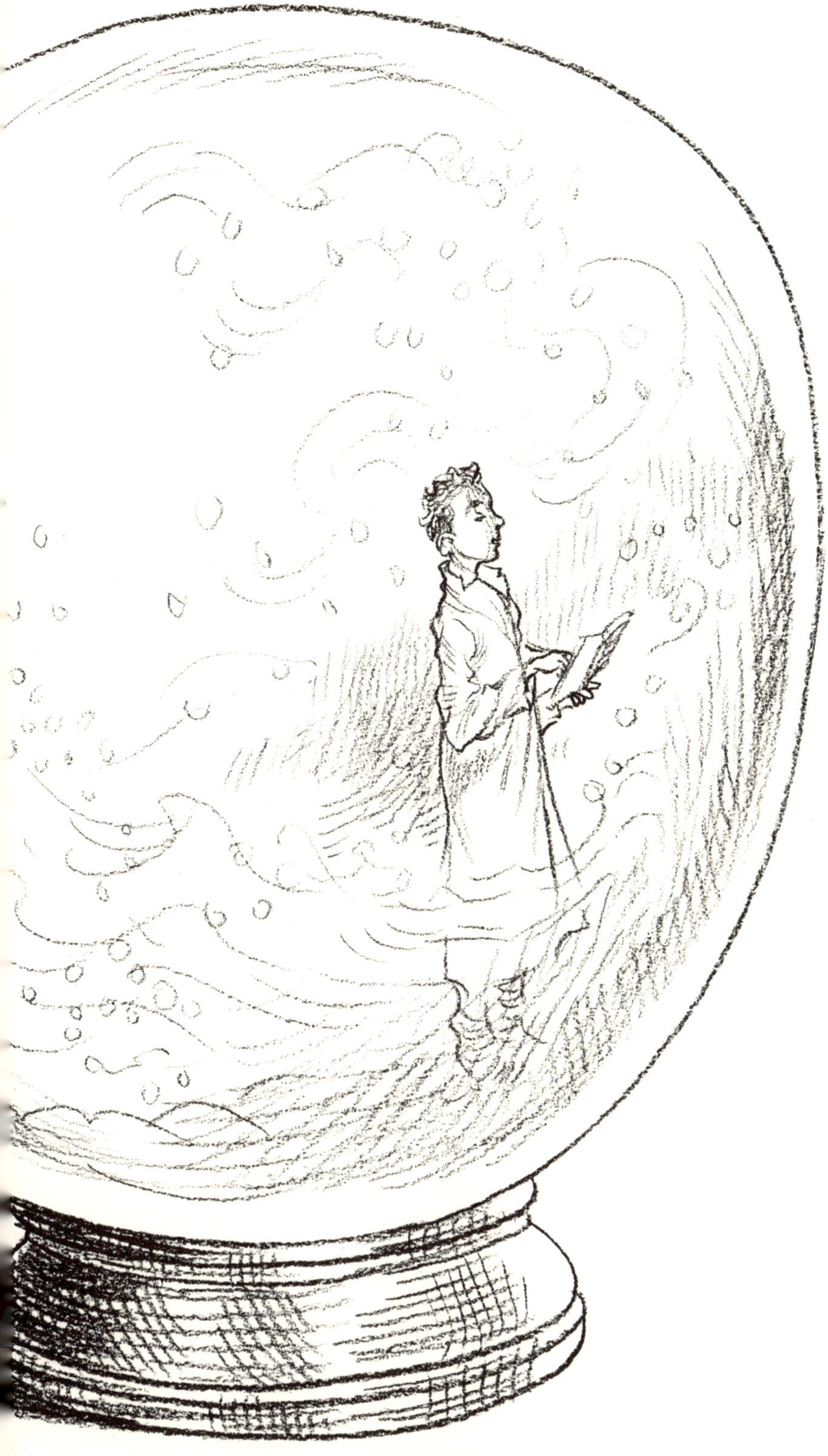

Acknowledgements

. . . and this time, I'm allowed more than fifty words!

I'll forever be grateful to my publisher, Sarah Pakenham, for seeing something in my work and reaching out. With that first email, Sarah, you started, truly, the most exciting adventure. Without people like you taking a chance on new voices, the world is a quieter place. Thank you for all you've done, and I can't imagine a better first home for my words. To me, Scallywag Press is Simply Perfect.

Janice Thomson, my editor, is a sparkling powerhouse of experience and clear heart. This book owes so much to you, Janice. I believe we make quite the "exquisite" team.

To be told that Chris Riddell is illustrating your debut collection! To see those illustrations for the first time! To know you'll hold them in your heart forever! Chris, your art hasn't just broken the word limit by adding a thousand words to each poem, it's elevated this book beyond words.

I began this project – working title: The Fifties – in 2014, and for being some of its earliest ears, I'd like to thank Evelyn Forsyth, Elaine Furmage, Craig Martin, Callum Stephen and, of course, Joan Mills, my "mummy's mum". In more recent times, I've also been grateful for the encouragement and advice of Richard Bramwell, Richard Smith, Margaret Tomlinson and Xavier Martin Valladares. To my biggest (and longest-standing) supporters – being my parents, Jane and Nigel Lamb – my heart's thanks. You gave me the space to finish this collection when the world was ending and were always there when I held it to your ears. x

I'm fascinated by the sheer possibility of poetry, where a whole universe can be offered to the reader in a precisely-chosen packet of words (in this case, exactly fifty!). Dear reader, thank you for reading this book and exploring the many universes the people on these pages helped me construct, hone and present to you. They are now yours, for passing on. — SL

About the Poet

SIMON LAMB is a poet, performer and storyteller. With a background in teaching, he works extensively in schools to ignite and inspire young learners by sharing his passion for poetry. He has lived on the west, east and north coasts of Scotland, never far from the sea, and currently lives in Ayrshire, where he is the Scriever, the writer-in-residence at the Robert Burns Birthplace Museum, 2022–2025.
A Passing On of Shells is Simon's debut collection of poetry.

About the Illustrator

CHRIS RIDDELL, the 2015–2017 UK Children's Laureate, is an award-winning illustrator and acclaimed political cartoonist. He is currently the only artist to have won the Kate Greenaway Medal three times. He has illustrated the work of many celebrated children's authors, and has long-loved working with poetry, illustrating several books by former Poet Laureate Ted Hughes early in his career. He lives in Brighton with his family.

About the Publisher

SCALLYWAG PRESS was founded in 2018, with the aim of publishing books that entertain and engage young readers. We love books where words and pictures both play their different parts to convey moments of drama, emotion and humour. We love books that reflect on our lives and provide valuable perspectives which could be useful to readers of any age. We love books as beautiful objects. *A Passing On of Shells* is our first book of poetry.